Nicky

A Memoir

By Dominic Missimi

The characters in *Nicky: A Memoir* are real. They are Dominic Missimi's family members, friends, and acquaintances. The settings and place names also are real.

ISBN 9798681760870 (paperback)

Nicky

A Memoir

By Dominic Missimi

Mangia bene, ridi spesso, amo molto

Eat well, laugh often, love much

An old Italian proverb and Nicky's recipe for life

Nicky: A Memoir is dedicated to the memory of my parents,
Gaetano and Arcangela Missimi.

New Lexington
Ohio
IT'S WHERE MY STORY
BEGINS

ACKNOWLEDGEMENTS

Nicky: A Memoir would not have been possible without the extraordinary assistance of two talented women. First, my heartfelt thanks to Pam Mayers, who inspired me to write this memoir. In 2018, I enrolled in a class Pam taught called "Guided Autobiography." In this class, I first read my opening chapters aloud. Pam encouraged me to continue writing the personal essays that eventually would become this book.

My second angel is Alison Sneider, a Detroit-era friend of nearly 50 years, who loved me enough to volunteer to edit my manuscript. We began across a dining room table in Florida, where my wife Nancy and I spend the winter and where Alison came for a January vacation. Laptops facing one another, we organized the chapters and started editing. Since returning to our Midwest and New England lives, we have spent more than 100 hours in phone calls, emails, and Zoom meetings, going over the manuscript many times, checking facts, and cataloguing photos. I am immensely grateful for her attentive, creative, grammatical, and patient contributions to my little book. I'm not sure I could have done this without her. Or, if I did manage it, it wouldn't be nearly so polished. She is indeed a special friend.

I also am grateful to several other special angels—the talented artist Gerry Pearson Nichols, who created the map of my hometown neighborhood and other illustrations, and my equally talented cousin Mary Circelli, who not only located many of the photos used here but took some of them as well. Michael Byrne contributed his expertise in the layout and production of the book.

Tony Andrade lent his artistry to the creation of the cover design. Ben Finley offered his IT skills in formatting and problem-solving the final manuscript. And Geoffrey Edwards fashioned the family trees.

Of course, there would be no *Nicky: A Memoir* without my Italian-American family who came to the U.S. from Sicily and Puglia to settle in Ohio. My story is their story.

And what is a memoir without recollections of my boyhood neighbors and friends plus my adult family, friends, former students, and colleagues?

Grazie, tutti.

Dominic Missimi, 2020

TABLE OF CONTENTS

PART TWO: *CRESCERE* (Grown Up)

INTRODUCTION

Thirty years ago, I decided to celebrate my Italian-American heritage by writing a film script, titled *Under the Arbor*. My good friends Richard and Nancy Kordos, classmates from the University of Detroit, founded a Chicago casting company. They had great success casting one of their first feature films, *The Fugitive*, which starred Harrison Ford and Tommy Lee Jones and achieved considerable popularity.

It wasn't long before Nancy Kordos asked me, "Why don't we try to get your script produced?"

We didn't have much success. While we all had major contacts with Hollywood producers and directors, our script appeared at a time when Italian-American based stories had saturated the market. *Moonstruck*, *Rocky*, *Saturday Night Fever*, and a never-ending parade of mobster movies and TV shows had cornered the public's interest in immigrant America. Audiences weren't looking for another Mediterranean mother stirring spaghetti sauce while her handsome husband took off his wedding ring for a night with his *cumpahs.* There was little interest in a coming-of-age tale of a young Italian-American boy growing up in a dying coal-mining town in southeastern Ohio, dreaming of a career in the bright lights of New York City.

Like my film script, *Nicky* is a story about an Italian family who came to America. It's special to me because I lived it, and it unfolded in a very special corner of the world.

My life is not unique. I have read countless pieces of fiction by talented Italian-American writers who bring to life memorable casts of characters and recount a charming collection of unforgettable stories of their Italian families. With every delicious detail I find myself smiling as I recognize my *nonni* (grandparents) and a complete gallery of my parents, aunts, uncles, brothers, sister, and dozens of *le miei cugini* (my cousins).

I'm not a poet, with an endless collection of metaphors and pithy quotes to make my text sparkle. I write in plain-speak—like I'm having a chat. I grew up in a house with a family who spoke Italian throughout the day, saving their English for the milkman, the postman, and their kids. As my mom often said, "We don't talk fancy." I'm her son, for sure.

I hope you will enjoy *Nicky* as you travel through the pages of my life. I've been delighted to be your guide on this journey of seven decades and am grateful to all who have agreed to travel with me through my *dolce vita.*

PART ONE

Il Ragazzo

(The Boy)

LA FAMIGLIA

In the last minute of the movie *Moonstruck*, the camera pans to a sepia-toned antique photo of the Castorini family, the major characters of the film. The camera pans in even closer as the audience hears a voice saying "*la famiglia.*"

Every Italian-American watching the film understands the ultimate importance of that final moment. *Famiglia* is everything, the most important aspect of life. Everything grows up from it and everything turns back to it. It is the center of the universe.

The Missimi *famiglia* was a ragtag collection of characters from a boisterous 1950s southern Italian movie, transferring all the grit and poverty from the streets of Naples and Palermo to a southern

Ohio landscape of farms and coal mines where poor, immigrant families scratched out a living.

The house I grew up in was inhabited by two *famiglie*—the Missimis plus my mother's parents, the DePintos. The Missimis came from Sant'Agata di Militello on the northern coast of Sicily and the DePintos from a small town outside Bari in the region of Apulia. These two families settled at 714 North Main Street in the southeastern Ohio village of New Lexington and it was the center of our world. Our neighbors also were immigrants, from Lebanon, and together they created the most delicious scents wafting over the hills of Perry County: bubbling tomato sauce rich with basil and oregano and the Middle Eastern aromas of lemon, cumin, cinnamon, and mint—a remarkable sensory experience.

Pietro and Vittoria (Victoria) DePinto were the patriarch and matriarch of our household. Their daughter, Arcangela (Archangel), was my mother, though everyone called her Angie. Angie married Sicilian Gaetano (Guy) Missimi and they raised five children in the house, including the youngest, Domenico—that's me. For the 18 years I lived at 714 North Main, though, I was Nicky.

My parents managed the household, while my grandparents moved through the space like visiting guests or minor royalty.

The two men in the house were quite similar and probably very similar to other immigrant Italian men in the 1950s. They had little to say, did not involve themselves in matters of the household or even their children, and preferred to talk among themselves, play cards, and drink homemade "dago red." My father never attended my football games or watched me star in the school play. There seemed to be some unwritten rule that for southern Italian men, showing interest in and affection for a son was unmanly. Theirs was a simple existence of long workdays, early suppers (we never said "dinner"—that was for rich people), cowboy movies on the 17-inch TV set, and early to bed.

On the other hand, the women were the backbone of the home and had lots to say. Life began and ended with *la mamma.* Mine was up at 4:30 a.m. to prepare her husband's breakfast before he climbed aboard his truck for a 12-hour day of driving loads of coal and sand. The rest of her day was a non-stop flurry of cleaning, cooking, and brewing pot after pot of coffee for the neighbors who stopped in for a daily visit.

She tended the garden and washed the clothes in her old Maytag machine under the hanging grapes of the enormous arbor attached to the house, which also was the center of the neighborhood's social life. She baked bread, canned tomato sauce for a year's worth of pasta, and prepared a major meal that must be waiting on the table as her husband walked through the door at 4:30 p.m. Mom's was a 12-hour day, too.

The other woman who lived in our house was my grandmother Victoria. She did nothing. She was the *imperatrice* (empress). In her calico house dress and never-matching apron, she sat hour after hour in her overstuffed chair, shaped very much like her overstuffed body. She watched TV endlessly and only raised her voice to give commands.

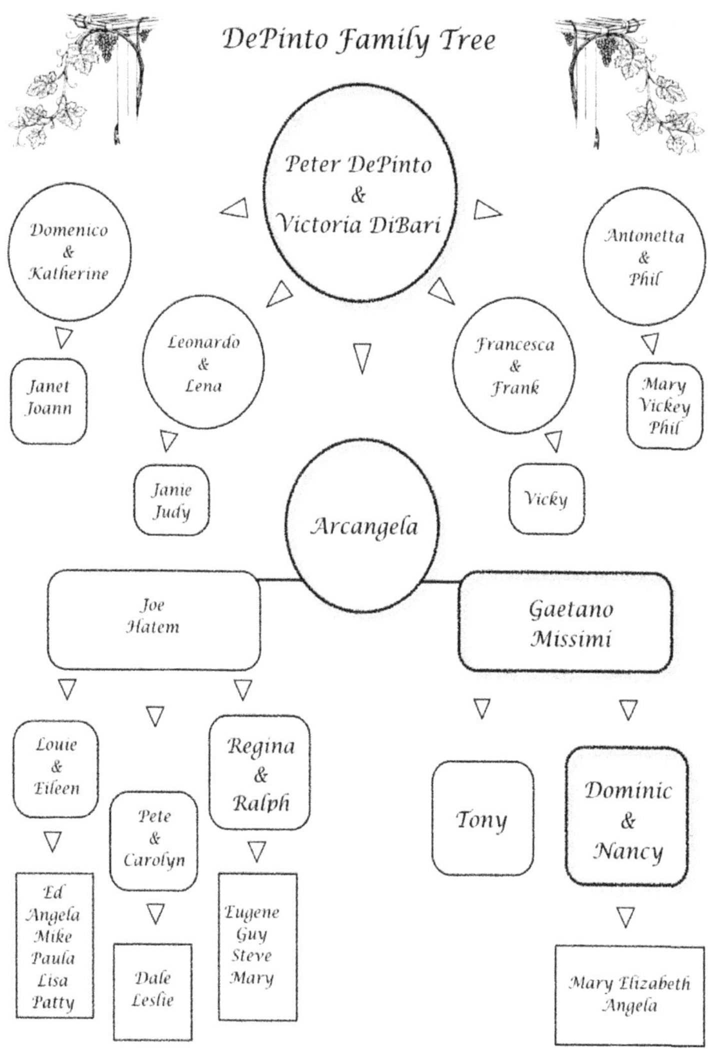
DePinto Family Tree
Peter DePinto & Victoria DiBari
Domenico & Katherine
Antonetta & Phil
Leonardo & Lena
Francesca & Frank
Janet Joann
Mary Vickey Phil
Janie Judy
Vicky
Arcangela
Joe Hatem
Gaetano Missimi
Louie & Eileen
Pete & Carolyn
Regina & Ralph
Tony
Dominic & Nancy
Ed Angela Mike Paula Lisa Patty
Dale Leslie
Eugene Guy Steve Mary
Mary Elizabeth Angela

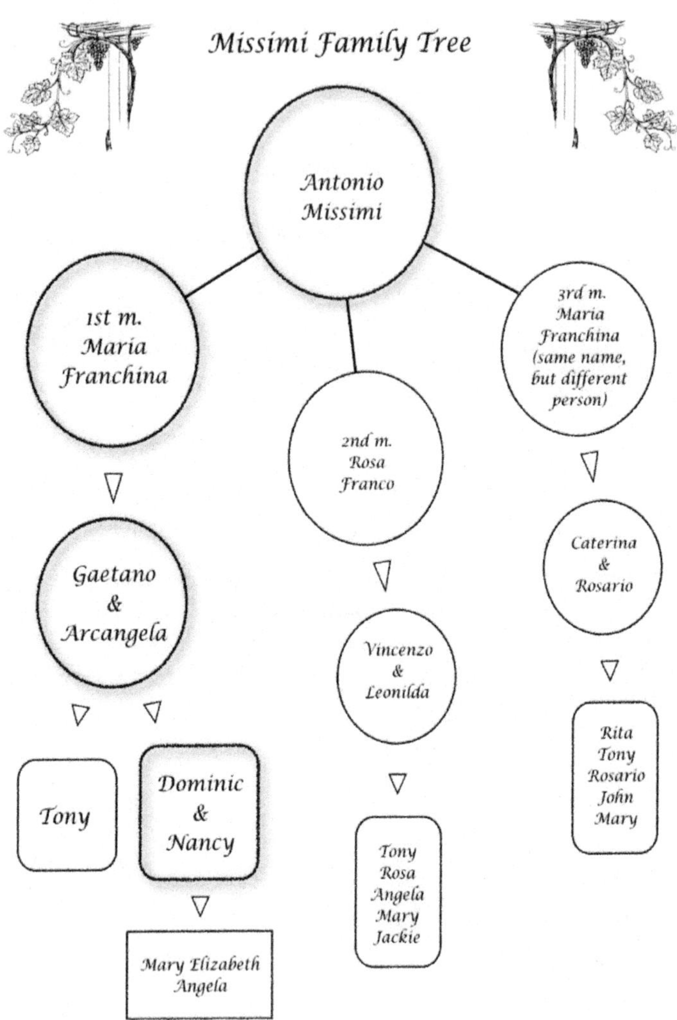
Missimi Family Tree
Antonio Missimi
1st m. Maria Franchina
2nd m. Rosa Franco
3rd m. Maria Franchina (same name, but different person)
Gaetano & Arcangela
Vincenzo & Leonilda
Caterina & Rosario
Tony
Dominic & Nancy
Mary Elizabeth Angela
Tony Rosa Angela Mary Jackie
Rita Tony Rosario John Mary

"*Domenico, vieni qui*!" [Come here!] And off I ran to be at her beck and call, changing the station, bringing her coffee with an anise cookie, and scratching her back. Like her husband, grandma said very few words. In fact, in her 60 years living in the U. S. she possessed a 20-word English vocabulary. Her husband, Grandpa Pete, however, had only 10. Let's hope they understood more than they spoke, since grandma spent all day watching American TV.

Italian was the first language of my household, but I refused to attempt to speak it. I was an American. I was embarrassed to be a first-generation Italian, much less a kid just off the boat like Joey Pacino. I was in charge of escorting Joey to his first day at Saint Rose of Lima Elementary School. He and his family had just arrived from Sicily. When Joey pulled out his sandwich for lunch, it was homemade bread piled high with slices of onion. I was humiliated. My peanut butter and jelly was what American kids ate, not some foul-smelling "Italian" onion sandwich!

Our house was unusual for four reasons.

First of all, most of the acre lot was an enormous garden, overseen by my grandpa, who brought a sprout of a fig tree to his new country and constantly nursed, hovered over, and cajoled the poor thing to take root and stay alive. The majority of the garden was devoted to tomatoes—from beefsteak and cherry to many varieties used for canning sauce for pasta. There were green peppers and hot peppers, several kinds of lettuce, green beans, potatoes, eggplant, watermelon, and cantaloupe, as well as zucchini. Some of the zucchini were of the "baseball bat" variety, four to five feet long, dangling overhead and supported by the grape arbor.

The arbor itself was enormous. It was about 16 feet wide by 80 feet long, a continuous awning of sweet smelling red and green grapes, waiting to be snipped in mid-August for the annual wine-making, supervised by Grandpa Pete and his Italian compadres. Under the leafy bower of grape vines, the entire Italian-American and Lebanese community spent countless evening hours enjoying my mother's hospitality, as she bustled in and out through the screened door to bring more coffee, cookies, and cake.

The shrine was the second-most-memorable feature of our house. Built at the edge of the garden, midway between our house and my sister Regina's, was the shrine to Saint Theresa of Avila. My mom made an arrangement with Marion Procacci, my godfather and New Lexington's resident mason, to erect a shrine to the memory of her granddaughter, little Theresa, who died from Sudden Infant Death Syndrome. This was not a simple little shrine like you'd see in the yards of immigrant families. This was church-sized. I think it would have been a good location for Bernadette or the children of Fatima to experience an apparition. Made of brown sandstone, the shrine was studded with large pieces of sparkling, colored glass and bits of pink pottery from the famous southeastern Ohio pottery companies.

Poor Saint Theresa eventually was replaced by the Italian favorite, Saint Anthony, at about the same time my brother Tony was ordained a priest. I always believed my mom was secretly hoping he might at least become a bishop, if he wasn't going to be the Pope.

Our living room was the third most memorable stop on any tour of the Missimi *casa.* My mom decorated it in a style that I discovered much later would become the height of "camp." The draperies were chartreuse and deep red, like most of the furniture and accessories, printed with large bird of paradise flowers and gigantic stalks of bamboo. You know. You've seen this fabric in every vintage clothing store with a special 1950s section. Our furniture was exotic, to say the least. The luxuriously tufted couch was the same deep red, with heavy six-inch fringe, and the occasional chairs were chartreuse brocade. All the furniture featured hand-crocheted, pineapple-patterned doilies placed on the backs, made by my mom. She spent hours starching them, with the help of tomato paste cans to give the doilies those stiff, white waves. Everyone was careful about settling into the furniture to avoid neck lacerations.

Best of all were the two large ceramic lamps that stood on either side of the couch. They were Nubian slaves (offensive today, but not uncommon back then), in pink harem pants and floral turbans. Their arms strained over their heads and held enormous pink fans—which, of course, lit up. I never knew how to describe my mother's taste in decorating. I guess it was "dago chic."

What made 714 North Main unlike any other house on the wrong side of the tracks was its physical attachment to the beer joint, Whitey's Tavern—the fourth leg of the Missimi house tour. The smell of my mom's delicious sauce bubbling away on the stove sometimes competed with the smell of stale beer and old grease sizzling on the bar's kitchen grill. Whitey's was the favorite spot of the Kentucky miners who went there to blow their paychecks and let off steam. On hot summer evenings I peered through my bedroom window at the cars parked on Mechanic Street, the alley next to my house, glad that I was not a child locked in a car while my parents downed their beers and plugged the jukebox with nickels and dimes to hear their favorite country and western tunes.

Fannie White was the proprietress of the establishment. She was a kind lady, and mom often paid her to bake magnificent hams for our holiday celebrations. She could make them look like a magazine cover—with circles of pineapple, maraschino cherries, and cloves pressed into the ham in perfect rows. If only her beer joint was as appealing as her ham!

This was *mio mondo*—my world.

When I studied acting in college, I most enjoyed the exercises involving sense memory, perhaps because all my memories of growing up in New Lexington ("New Lex" for short) are deeply rooted in sensory experiences. I easily can recall the sweet smell of the arbor grapes as I stared across the expanse of our beautiful garden. I can smell the basil I dropped into the pots of tomatoes as I helped mom make sauce ("gravy") for a year's worth of pasta. I can hear the freight trains as they passed near my bedroom window and feel the heat from my sunburned shoulders as I squirmed on the clean, bleached sheets. I can smell my mom's "Here's My Heart" Avon perfume and my own Old Spice shaving lotion as I splashed it on before a big date. I can smell my sister's delicious peanut butter fudge and mom's pizza and bread baking in the oven. My world was a celebration of sights and sounds and scents—the tastes and touches of the ingredients that were my recipe for life.

THE LAY OF THE LAND

We lived on Monument Square, a small, seldom-looked-after parcel on the wrong side of the tracks. Descending the "straight hill" led to the epicenter of all my favorite haunts. The monument was dedicated to the local soldiers who died in the two World Wars. It was a relatively unimpressive memorial, shaped like a cross with the names of dozens of young men chiseled into the stone marker.

Four small, immigrant-owned businesses surrounded the square. (There's a color map of Monument Square on the back cover.)

Hatem's Confectionary was a popular hangout for young people, with an enormous rack of comic books, a long, old-fashioned soda fountain counter serving shakes, banana splits, and "tombstone" sodas (with a shot of every syrup), and a rear door that led into Hatem's Television and Radio Repair.

The owners were our Lebanese friends, John and Nellie Hatem, and their sons and daughters who helped run both businesses. My mom was first married to Nellie's brother Joe. But his abusive treatment of her and their three children—my two half-brothers, Louie and Pete, and my half-sister, Regina—led to divorce. Having no education or religious training, my mom never realized that the result of the divorce would be excommunication. Father Donovan, our parish priest, came to the house to tell mom that she was no longer allowed to receive the sacrament of Holy Communion and her divorced status made her no longer a member of the Church. My mother was crushed. How could she be a sinner? She did it for the sake of her children!

Across the street from our house was Joe Pacino's Marathon gas station. Pepino, as we called him, was my family's good friend and he spent hours at our kitchen table downing cup after cup of my mom's thick, black coffee, which constantly perked on the ancient gas range. Joe had a strong-willed wife named Rosa who simply refused to speak a word of English, four strapping sons, one of whom was constantly being sent to the principal's office, and one daughter who, of course, was named Rosa.

The Lebanese Ellis family also lived on the square and ran a television and appliance shop. TVs were bought at Ellis's and fixed across the street at Hatem's. Their shop was a nightmare of disorganization, with hundreds of old washers, phonographs, radios, early-model TVs, and everything electrical strewn throughout the store. The best feature of the shop was the record section. This was the only place to buy the latest 45 rpms and it created a steady stream of young customers coming in and out for the new Elvis, Pat Boone, and Brenda Lee records.

The Triona family lived next to Hatem's Confectionary. Charlie Triona was the patriarch of his family and through his generosity and sponsorship he brought many of my family members to America. He helped give my grandfather his first job and he brought my dad to America when he was a young boy. His daughter Lucy was my mom's best friend and the two women spent hours chatting over coffee and complaining about their live-in parents. Lucy had "rooms to let" and also ran a billiard room attached to her house, just as the tacky Whitey's Tavern was attached to ours.

My mom always marveled over Lucy's beautiful complexion. "Just look at her skin! Not a wrinkle! How the hell does she do that?" She said that every time we ran into Lucy. She was so impressed with the fact that Lucy never put water on her face. She cleaned only with cold cream—no soap and water.

Two other Monument Square businesses were run by non-immigrants. Across the street from our house was Wade Kimball's Jack Sprat Valley Market, a run-down grocery and hardware store where my mom sent me regularly for bread, milk, and butter, though I spent hours picking out penny candy, my favorite maple Bun Bars, ice cream sandwiches, orange sherbet Skyrockets, and ice-cold grape pop. I loved saying "Just put it on the bill, Wade!" It always made me feel like we were rich and we could buy anything with those seven little words. Wade just chomped on a large chunk of bologna from his unappetizing meat case. "Say hi to your mom, Nicky!" he shouted after me.

Dunkle's was at the opposite end of the square from our house. It was another tavern, much nicer than the cockroach-infested Whitey's. Dunkle's was popular with the locals, with a loud juke box that blared past midnight. It attracted a much younger crowd than the Kentucky miners who frequented Whitey's. High schoolers patronized the front, where only food was served (primarily burgers and fries). It was the one teenage hangout for young people who lived in the valley, not on the hill where the more well-to-do residents lived.

Walking out the front door of Dunkle's and turning left on Broadway guaranteed an arrival at the Hatem's house. As a young boy I loved running vegetables from our garden to Nellie's kitchen, a gift from mom and grandpa. It was an exotic and messy place. A confusion of pots and pans and platters contained dozens of dishes-in-progress—some sitting on the stove, several spread across the kitchen table, and even more completed and cooling on the counter. Amid pots of mint and parsley and basil, there was tabbouleh salad (parsley, bulgur, and lemon), chickpea hummus, kibbeh (seasoned raw meat), fried falafel patties, and pans of baklava, the multi-layered honey dessert popular in Greece and throughout the Middle East. I mostly loved the stack of Lebanese bread, sprinkled with a distinctive spice called za'atar, a memorable mix of thyme, cumin, coriander, and other exotic ingredients. It had a magnificent fragrance and made the bread addictive. Nellie's kitchen always looked like the elaborate *antipasti* tables I later encountered in Italy when I ventured out to a more expensive "ristorante." It was a celebration for my nose; that kitchen was my favorite sense memory when I think of my childhood neighborhood.

Further down the street was the duplex house where my cousin Mary lived with Aunt Nee and Uncle Phil in one half and Aunt Fanny and Uncle Frank in the other.

Heading the opposite way out of Dunkle's led to my Uncle Dominic and Aunt Kate's house, and just a few houses further down Broadway was Uncle Leo and Aunt Lena's house. Kate and Lena were the two non-Italian members of the family. Both were colorful characters—lively and talkative local women who spoke with a pronounced southern Ohio twang. "I gotta go worsh the deeshes." "I'd love me a good feesh sangwitch." Most of my family had the same hillbilly accent, and my sister Regina often sounded like she was speaking a different language. Even my brother Tony still asks for a "salami and provolone sangwitch."

Looking back on it, it's ironic that I lived in New Lex for 18 years and never realized that the street of my dreams—Broadway—was just a block from my house on Monument Square. Today, Times Square, bisected by Broadway, is my favorite place to visit in New York and I have spent hundreds of hours watching fantastic theatre on the Great White Way. My childhood Broadway, on the other hand, had no theatres or bright lights—just four gas stations, a bowling alley, three bars, a dry cleaner, an itsy-bitsy food market and a junk yard. My mom always liked to tell me "*E cosi che va, Nicolino*!" [That's the way it is, little Nicky!]

THE CAST OF CHARACTERS

Pete DePinto

My *nonno* (grandfather) was Pietro (Pete). His last name should have been DiPinto but, as is the case with so many immigrants, they were at the mercy of the folks at Ellis Island whose job it was to translate names to English; often, the names clearly typed on passports were poorly transcribed.

Pete was the patriarch. He and his wife Victoria had a dozen children, but only five survived—Domenico, Leonardo, Francesca, Antonetta, and Arcangela, my mom. I always thought it was extremely cool to have a mother named Archangel, like Saint Michael and Saint Gabriel that we learned about in religion class.

Pete DePinto lived for 83 years but never set foot inside a school. Just like his wife, he could barely write his name. He knew numbers, he knew a few weather words, a few food words, but what he knew best was swear words. "Sunamabeech!" was his favorite.

Pete was six feet tall and weighed more than 200 pounds, with a large head of balding grey hair, more wire-like than human. Most distinctive was his singed moustache, worn in the style of a young Benito Mussolini (or even a little bit like Adolf Hitler).

It was astonishing that he had any hair under his lip at all. Pete favored pungent, Italian cigars—"stogies," we called them. At Christmas, it was his only gift: four boxes under the tree to last him for the next 12 months. He cut each cigar into eight pieces. Lighting these butt-sized pieces, nestled completely under his moustache, was a pyrotechnic wonder. Each match flame was followed by "Goddam sunamabeech!" plus the smell of burning hair. The lighting of the cigar was limited to three times a day: once in the morning with a cup of

espresso, while watching TV in the evening, and sometimes right before bed. Otherwise, the cigar stayed perched and ready for fire, never moving from his mouth for the entire day.

Pete also was famous for his clothes. He wore a pair of bib overalls every day of his life. And an ancient flannel shirt. He had a closet full of them, and they were worn until they practically fell off. "Give me those goddam clothes!" my mom yelled at him. "I'm going to burn them!" He hated the thought of having something new and preferred to wear clothes like a second skin. Unfortunately, the downside of this was that the smell of the cigar-infused overalls preceded his arrival into any room.

Grandpa was unquestionably the worst driver in New Lex. No one wanted to be behind Pete's battered 1953 Ford. Every morning throughout high school, he drove my cousin Mary and me to Saint Aloysius Academy (St. Al's). We sank deep into the back seats as cars behind us tried to honk grandpa off the road. "*Fongoul*!" he shouted through the window at the car-honkers. It was a variation on the Italian "f" word and it came in second only to "sunamabeech!" Mary and I were used to his profanity. It was part of his essence. He seldom reached a speed of 20 mph, and only on a few occasions do I remember him shifting into second gear, let alone third. He seldom obeyed street signs. "Grandpa, that was a stop sign!"

"You see someone come? No need stop!" So he didn't.

Life is full of mysteries. The fact that grandpa, Mary, and I escaped bodily injury is a miracle and the fact that he never had his license taken away is an even bigger one. The real miracle is how he ever got a license in the first place.

Most people were afraid of grandpa. Townspeople accused him of poisoning their cats. He had that look of a male *strega nona*, the legendary Italian witch made famous by Tomie dePaola, who wrote and illustrated a series of children's books on this hook-nosed, prominently-chinned witch doctor. But the townspeople didn't know Grandpa Pete the way I did. He was a gentle soul, obsessing over his garden and grape vines, arguing with his friend Joe Triona about who loved his wife more, babysitting his great-grandchildren as they rode their trikes under the arbor and most of all, keeping his fig tree alive, the one he brought from the old country and planted in the ground on Main Street. He believed if he could keep it alive, all would be well in his new home in America.

Victoria DePinto

Grandma Victoria DePinto was the reigning monarch and martyr in our house and held court from her easy chair in the living room. From early morning until late at night, she sat there. Through family catastrophes, childbirths, natural disasters, she sat there. If she needed something, she knew someone would come to serve her. Usually it was me, her little Nicky.

Every morning she mustered enough energy to get up from the chair and make my favorite breakfast. It was a mug of hot coffee diluted with steaming milk, with bits of broken, stale bread and tons of sugar sprinkled on top. I called it "sapooch." I never knew why.

Grandma was heavy like her husband. She had fine brown hair streaked with grey, and it hung to her waist. She washed it only a few times a year, at the same time she was given a bath by her daughters—an actual sit-in-the-tub kind, not the sponge bath she preferred. Like most poor western Europeans, my grandparents had done without showers and baths in the old country. They considered them frivolous and unnecessary, only for the rich.

The martyrdom of Grandma Victoria was most obvious at mealtime. "Mom, get up! Come to the table! Supper's ready," my mom shouted from the kitchen.

"No. I no hungry. You eat."

And so we did, all of us around the table devouring mom's delicious pasta while Grandma sat in her overstuffed chair. To maintain her image of suffering, she'd had to find her sustenance beforehand and away from the kitchen table. She was a crafty thief. On one of her trips to the bathroom before dinner, grandma would drag through the kitchen and stop at the stove where a large pot was bubbling with the sauce and meatballs for the evening meal. She'd check to make sure no one could see her. Faster than anyone could say "Stop, thief!" she'd plunge gnarled fingers into the simmering sauce and pull out a meatball, slap it into her handkerchief, and glide through the bathroom door. When she returned to her easy chair, tomato sauce rimmed her lips and she was ready to refuse dinner. "Come to the table, Mamma," my mom pleaded.

"You eat. I no hungry," she said, smacking her lips.

Grandma and Grandpa and their five children (Angie on right)

Grandma also was a night-time thief, not stealing meatballs but money. I spent many nights sitting in front of the TV after everyone had gone to sleep. Once she heard her husband snoring away in their antique bed, she appeared in the living room, which adjoined their bedroom, dragging behind her my grandpa's bib overalls.

For a woman who complained about her fingers being too arthritic to tie her apron or button her dress, at midnight they moved like Liberace at the keyboard as she yanked a wad of greenbacks from grandpa's pockets. Without making a sound, she removed the rubber band that held the bills together. I watched her without taking my eyes off the TV screen, and even with sideways glances I could see her peel away a dollar bill and slip it into her enormous bra. She could have put a hundred bills in that bra and no one ever would have noticed, but she had simple needs. Just as smoothly, she slipped back to her bedroom with tiny, quiet little steps—like a Geisha dancer.

When Grandma Victoria died and my mom and Aunt Nee cleaned out her meager possessions, they discovered a metal box in the back of her closet. It contained close to $2,000. I have no doubt that Grandpa Pete knew all about it. He probably didn't want to spoil the most exciting five minutes of her day.

Perhaps my greatest memory of grandma has to do with her farts. We were sitting in our living room—Tony and I on the floor—watching *The Voice of Firestone*. My parents were on the couch, my grandpa in his favorite easy chair with the standing ashtray next to him for his evening stogie, and Grandma Victoria squeezed into her upholstered chair. It was a breathless minute when she'd lower herself to land on the cushion and we were much relieved when we heard the chair groan at its sudden burden.

We hated that show but my dad insisted we watch it. After all, a great deal of the program featured famous arias by the most beloved Italian composers, sung by stars from the Metropolitan

Opera, mostly Italians. I never knew if it was the fact that they were singing in Italian or the beauty of the music, but my coal-miner dad often sat there with tears rolling down his cheeks. Occasionally, there was even a sob. Tony and I were bored, as usual, but little did we know how Victoria would light up our evening.

Ever so slowly, she powered herself up to her feet, which normally meant it was time to use the bathroom. Unfortunately, that meant a trip across the center of the living room, through the kitchen, and a final arrival in the tiny half-bath. As she balanced herself after her heavy-breathing ascent to her feet, she took the first step. With that came the grotesque sound of a whoopy cushion—a long, drawn-out splat of a fart that rocked the room. Tony and I rolled over and stared at her in disbelief. But nothing was going to impede her progress to that bathroom. With each step came another splatty bit of flatulence. Worse yet, she had decided to shorten the distance by stepping over the bodies of her grandsons.

Don't move! we both were thinking. If we tripped her up, a great mass of flesh would descend on us and it could be the end of the Missimi brothers! We didn't smell anything, but the sound of her machine-gun farts sent us into hysterical laughter. With each step "rat-a-tat-tat" came out of her butt!

"*Gesu, Maria*, Mom!" my mother shouted. "Couldn't you get up sooner?"

"*Che fai*, Vittoria?" grandpa asked, choking on his stogie.

"That goddam woman is going to be the death of me!" my dad yelled, even though he was joining his sons in the laughter.

She continued her journey, with nary a word spoken. I was sure she was going to lose it—literally. But the bathroom door closed just as the chubby Italian tenor reached the climax of "*Nessun Dorma*" from *Turandot*. "*Vincero, vincero*!" he sang dramatically. "I will conquer, I will conquer!" as my grandmother slammed onto the toilet seat.

Don't get me wrong. I loved my Grandma Victoria. She was filled with mischief in her old age, as well as a bit too much gas, but she loved her "Nicootz" and I never tired of being her little helper, her little translator. Though I didn't speak Italian, I could understand my grandparents' southern Italian dialect, so I always was called to grandma's side to deliver messages to mom and grandpa. Though grandma clearly was a comedic star in my life, she always played second banana to the virtuosic performances of her daughter, my mom.

Arcangela Eleanora (DePinto) Missimi—"Angie"

And now to the star of the "world of Nicky"—Angie, my mom, the girl with one buttock. But more on that later.

My mom was a svelte and lovely bride on her wedding day: a petite size 4 with marcelled hair, dressed in a white lace sheath that was pure Gatsby. However, I knew her as a size 22 with motherly bosoms, fine brown hair that was softly curled, and beautiful fair skin (though not to be compared with the remarkable, wrinkleless face of Lucy Triona). My mom had a long list of attributes that made her one of New Lex's most charming and colorful characters.

It is important to understand Angie's manner of delivery. She spoke very loudly. VERY LOUDLY. Add to that decibel level a constant spattering of swear words (which she picked up from the truckers who worked with my dad) and a litany of quaint expressions. When my friends visited the house for the first time, my mom often shocked them when she yelled at me.

"Come here, you little bastard. I'm gonna beat your ass when I get my hands on you!" While she spared us the "f" word (and so did my dad) she had a full arsenal of swear words, often forgetting who was in the room—including our priest, Father Donovan, who once dropped his coffee cup during one of my mom's colorful conversations.

She loved including many of her favorite expressions in her monologues. "Burn your ass, you sit on the blister." "If you make your bed, you have to sleep in it." "She thinks her ass is a pineapple and everyone wants a bite." When she was worried about my interest in a theatre career, she always put me in my place with "You'll never be able to build me a shit house!"

Angie was dearly loved. She was an infinitely kind person and the warmest hostess imaginable. She simply would not take "no" for an answer when offering coffee, food, a night's lodging, or help in any situation. She was a perfect example of "the Italian style." It was the kind and generous quality found in every southern Italian family. Angie's greatest joy in life was her role as a hostess. A constant parade of neighbors and friends stopped by the house from 7 in the morning until 10 at night. Sometimes she made seven pots of coffee a day for her guests, though she never stopped her work when they dropped in. She continued washing clothes, breading pork chops, canning tomatoes, baking a cake—she brought everyone into her workaday world. She often discovered three coffee cups she had strewn around the house while she worked and entertained. She was a master of tasks and talk.

One annual occurrence provided an opportunity to see Arcangela Missimi in all her glory as a gracious hostess and out-of-control house manager. One never knew when it would occur, but it always happened in the same way.

She came running into the house, holding the mail. "Nicky! I need you to read this letter! Come here and help your mom!" When I arrived she stared at me with such intensity that I was sure she was holding a death notice.

"They're coming," she announced. "Those goddam freeloaders are coming!"

"What are you talking about, Ma?"

"I can read their names on the envelope. I know what it means." I quickly opened the letter and read the short message, written half in English and half in Italian. Though I was unable to figure out some words, I got the big phrases—"arrive April 3," "Easter weekend," "three-day stay," "God bless you and your family," and "love, Anthony and Rosa Mangiacavallo."

"The Mangiacavallos! Those damn mooches. They're coming next week—and they're going to ruin my big Easter dinner!"

Neither my grandparents nor my parents knew exactly who these two Clevelanders were. They were connected somehow to our Ohio relatives in Bellevue and Sandusky, and they had a definite connection to the Trionas down the street. But it had been a habit over the years that the wiry-haired couple would visit all their Italian friends throughout the Midwest, including the Missimis. I'm not sure they actually had a real home. They were always on the road and living out of their car, and there was never much talk about their kids.

"Why does God do this to me?" Angie moaned. "How am I gonna get through this? Your dad's gonna shit when he finds out they're coming."

My mom prided herself on being a model hostess, but the Mangiacavallos pushed all her buttons. Their imminent visit propelled everyone in the household, as well as my Aunt Nee and Aunt Fanny, to spend hours cleaning and polishing our humble little house from top to bottom. Bed linens and tablecloths were starched and pressed, dinner menus planned, bread baked, and canned tomatoes, peaches, and cherries brought up from the basement for special items on the Easter menu. For Good Friday mom prepared my dad's favorite dish—*baccala*—a dried, salted cod fish that she soaked in water for five days and baked with tomatoes, onions, olives, and capers. It was one of the very few exotic fish dishes I would eat, but I knew it would be an enormous hit with the house guests. They also were Sicilian, like my dad, and this was a favorite regional preparation.

Angie worked non-stop every day, making everything beautiful for the unwanted guests. She never missed a moment to complain about them to every neighbor who stopped by. Of course, she never failed to invite them back for coffee and cake once the guests arrived.

When finally the Mangiacavallos appeared at our doorstep, my mom effected a total transformation. She became the warmest and most hospitable hostess imaginable. And she wasn't putting on an act, though she was a consummate actress. She was sincere. She loved having guests in her house, people to make extra special meals for and people to fuss over. Every event in mom's life—Christmas and Easter dinners, family picnics, First Holy Communions—always elicited the same semi-hysterical reactions from her: "Dear God, when will this be over?!"

But when the moment arrived, she was in her glory. She was the prime mover and she delighted in hosting her big events as the woman in charge. She stood in her over-crowded kitchen, floral apron struggling to encircle her corpulence, long fork in one hand, wooden spoon in the other, conducting the symphony called "Angela's Easter Dinner" with the art and precision of Toscanini. Angie, smiling broadly at the Mangiacavallos, was thinking—if only you would visit every *other* year!

Angie Missimi played the role of the obedient and respectful wife of Guy Missimi, but she had strengths and convictions that would have made her a very modern 21st century woman. She guided my dad as he started his own trucking business, convincing a dealer in Columbus to sell dad his first truck without a down payment. She handled all business negotiations with his coal customers. She was a businesswoman at heart. And yet, like all the other immigrant women from the wrong side of the tracks, like all of my aunts, she never learned to drive. "That's for the men to do." That was one element of American life that their old-country beliefs couldn't change.

My mom counted on me for lots of things and we had a special mother/son understanding. I did anything she asked me to do and in return, she protected me from the anger of an exhausted dad who couldn't tolerate an idle son when he came home from work. "Your dad's pulling up in the truck, Nicky. You better get busy and not let him see you sitting around doing nothing!" I'd put down my magazine or hang up the phone and run outside to grab a bucket from the rain barrel and begin to water the tomato plants.

If dad caught me doing nothing it would be early curfew, no car, no allowance, or some other punishment for a lazy, good-for-nothing son. My mom always kept an eye out for me. In return, I helped her can tomatoes, bake pies, run the wet clothes through the ringer, go shopping and, on rare occasions (when my sister Regina was too busy), I even combed her hair so she could get to Mass on time.

I have more to say about mom when we spend a little time with her daughter, Regina, the apple who didn't fall far from the tree.

Gaetano Edgardo Missimi—"Guy"

My father was as slim as Angie on the day they were married. He looked like a young Edward G. Robinson in his double-breasted suit and white shoes. But most of his life he and Angie looked like matching salt and pepper shakers. They were both short and a little rotund, though Angie wore her excess pounds with jollity while my father wore his like a threat.

Dad was not a mean man. He didn't have time to be mean. He got up every morning at 4 and worked a 12-hour day, hauling coal in the winter and sand in the summer. He always was tired, but underneath it all, I think he was content with his life. He liked nothing better than getting home at 4:30, eating supper immediately, and settling in on the couch to watch the 5:30 cowboy serials with his father-in-law, Pete. If the weather was warm, he spent the rest of the daylight working in the garden with Pete and then enjoying his favorite chair under the grape arbor where mom served him coffee and Italian cookies.

He was a man of very few words, but what he said was clear and concise. His English was good, without a hint of an accent, even though he always spoke Italian with his in-laws and compadres. Whenever they didn't want my brother Tony and me to understand what they were saying—whether it was family gossip or a coming punishment—they switched to Italian. Dad spoke in his Sicilian dialect and mom in her Barese (from Bari) dialect. Over the years, they learned to understand each other and, for the most part, I could understand both of them.

Dad was menacingly terse and only spoke when he absolutely had to. He didn't speak to his kids. It didn't seem to matter to me and my brother Tony. It's just the way he was, or maybe the way all Italian fathers were. He did, however, enjoy a little name-calling. "Hey, *Chooch! Vieni qui*! [Hey, Jackass! Come here!], my dad often yelled. That also was Grandpa Pete's favorite name for me—*Chooch.* When I misbehaved, he also seemed to enjoy *disgraziato* (disgrace). And when he added "*gran* "' to the front of it, I was a "very big disgrace" to the family. These were their Italian endearments for little Nicky.

My only major contact with my dad was Saturday mornings in the winter when he hauled a load of coal to Columbus and I joined him. I inherited this horrible job from my older brothers, who had by then "graduated" from being junior coal haulers. By 6 a.m. we had loaded the truck at Sunnyhill Coal Mine in New Lex. For the drive to Columbus, I slept until dad shook me awake as he backed into the coal chute at the Town Apartments. I hated this job. The building had a miniscule boiler room and I had to shovel the entire load of coal as it came down the chute, pushing it back into the far corners of the sweltering room.

By 9 a.m. we had finished and I was numb, cold, and exhausted. No matter how much I blew my nose, out came a steady stream of black coal dust. I couldn't wait for a bath. What I really longed for was a shower, like the powerful ones in the locker room at St. Al's. We didn't have a shower in our house, so when I got home from coal-shoveling, I'd have to drain the tub at least three times to get rid of the scum and muck that had settled on the surface of the water.

Despite my need to be clean, I stifled it temporarily for a greater good: the treat my dad loved to give me, and I loved to receive, after a job well done. It was a trip to Burger Boy Drive In on Livingston Avenue, our favorite mid-morning pig-out—enormous double-decker burgers, fried chicken, and strawberry pie. I remember looking at my dad with my mouth unimaginably full and smiling at him with gratitude. He smiled back at me—a big grin. That was the most important approval he ever gave me. It was as close as I ever felt to my dad when I was a kid.

Regina Hatem Coffman

My half-sister Regina was 11 years older than I. I was much closer to her than to my two older half-brothers, Pete and Louis Hatem. They were, respectively, 12 and 15 years older.

I was very impressed with my brother Pete. I thought he was cool, a G.I. coming back to the house after having served overseas in Okinawa. Maybe I just loved the embroidered jacket he brought back for me. I also loved our trips to Columbus when I accompanied him in the truck to shovel coal at the apartment buildings—my apprenticeship before I took over the job from him. I felt like an adult when he talked to me about school and my friends.

My oldest brother Louis was a mystery. We never lived in the house together and seldom had a conversation until he was married and a father of six. I admired him for the wonderful father he had become, but we hardly knew each other.

Regina often served as my babysitter, even though she wasn't a very good one. She liked to talk endlessly and sometimes got distracted. Like the time she didn't see me fall off the swing and turned to look at me just as it was coming back to smack me on the forehead.

Bad babysitting aside, I loved being with Regina. I loved visiting her and husband Ralphie to make peanut butter fudge or sit in their living room watching TV with her family, chomping on buckets of popcorn and drinking my favorite RC Cola (I thought the pop was named for Ralph and Regina Coffman!). I loved helping her wrap my mom's hundreds of Christmas presents (mom insisted that every person in the family give a present to every other person in the family, even if only a pair of socks), with Regina letting me get a peek at what would be waiting for me under the tree.

There were times, however, I didn't like being with Regina. These were the occasions when I had to scrape Regina's family dinner off the kitchen ceiling. She'd lose track of the time talking on the phone and forget to shut off the pressure cooker. Because of this, beef stew was my least favorite family meal.

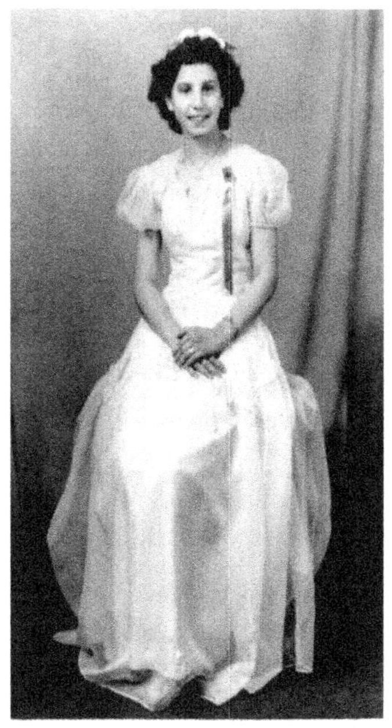

Regina was a perfect reproduction of her mother. If my mom had the power to take your breath away with her virtuosic display of idiosyncrasies, my sister Regina could make you faint dead away. She was one of the Lord's most unique creations. She was the embodiment of a hundred richly drawn characters, rolled into one spitting image of her mother, but wholly and completely her own unique self.

Together she and mom were unbeatable. They both talked at each other simultaneously, overlapping their lines. With the sheer volume of their speech—and boy, they could be loud!—along with their exuberant gesturing, their folksy expressions, and general sense of bravura acting technique, they were a five-act comedy being played under the leafy bough of our grape arbor.

Both my mom and my sister were great screamers. Screaming was part of their existence. We knew they were just talking, but visitors to our world would ask “Why are they screaming at each other?” They screamed when they hated something and they screamed when they loved someone. They screamed at As in religion and at Ds in conduct. They screamed at grandpa for not taking a bath and at me for taking too many. They screamed at grandma for living and for grandma when she died. They were comforting kinds of yells, as if only by truly exerting every muscle and pushing the words up and out could they convince everyone that they enjoyed living.

Though mom could not live without Regina, there were times when they would go for days without speaking, most often a disagreement over dad’s partiality for Regina over his own sons. Yet they loved each other in one of those classic mother/daughter relationships, both vying for the “most loved” award from the husband/father.

While Regina was dad’s stepdaughter, he loved her like one of his own. When she married neat little Ralph Coffman, dad threw her one of the biggest weddings New Lex had ever seen and built her a house behind our vegetable garden, about 100 yards from our back door. After a few years, he decided it wasn’t close enough, so he bought her the house next door.

After her four children had grown and Ralph passed away, Regina began to resemble mom. Her hair was equally as fine and she had my mom's same fair complexion. There may be something very true about how the human body—or the human spirit—deals with the loss of a loved one. After mom died, it seemed as if Regina's facial features began to reshape into the image of my mom. I got to see Regina's face for the last time in December 2018, as I knelt next to her coffin. How lovely that God would give us these two amazing women—Angie and Regina—the tree and the branch, both filled with unending kindness, eternal love for their families, heaps of theatricality, and having enough time to pour you another cup of coffee. How I loved them!

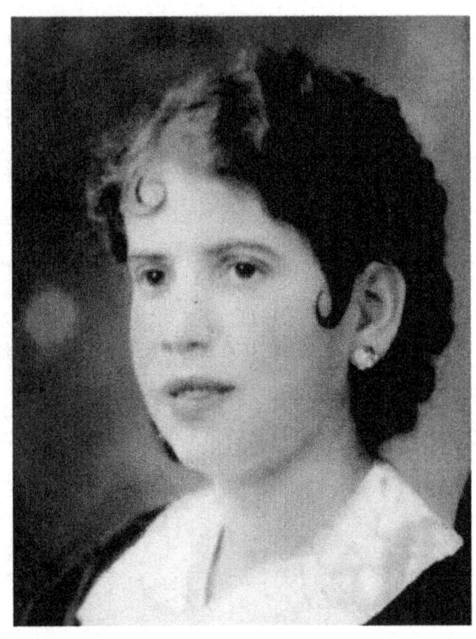

THE GIRL WITH ONE BUTTOCK

What was a poor Italian immigrant to do to make enough money to keep his family alive? It was a question Pete DePinto, my grandfather, asked himself over and over again in the 1920s. There was no work at the tile plant where a few of his compadres had found low-paying jobs working the ovens to create sewer tiles. While he had worked in the mines at Sunnyhill Coal, it had been months since he had been called up to burrow in the caves. But he had an idea how to solve this dilemma. His good friends, the Hatems, a large immigrant family from Lebanon, had found an easy way to make a quick buck, even if it was outside the law.

Abdullah Hatem lived in New Straitsville, Ohio. And he learned from his neighbors in that poor hillbilly community, where unemployment was normally 80 percent, that the one thing everyone seemed to want during Prohibition was booze—good old-fashioned, made-in-the-hills, burn-your-gullet moonshine. Bootlegging had been the major export of this small enclave of folks who lived outside the mainstream workforce. They could make good money with their homemade corn liquor, and God knows everyone needed some good money, including Abdullah's friend, Pete.

The two enterprising men decided it would be smarter to establish their business in the basement of Pete's home at 714 North Main. Who would suspect that these two men, who could speak barely a word of English, would have set up a still in the midst of the small community of Sicilian and Lebanese families?

But while their clandestine business helped pay for Pete's and Abdullah's rent and groceries and gave them a few extra bucks, it came at a price and would change my mom's life in a most dreadful way.

Little Angie DePinto was 12 years old. While her two brothers and two sisters spent their days in school, Angie, the oldest daughter, was pulled out of Saint Rose of Lima Elementary School after the third grade. Pete and Victoria needed her to help run the household. She learned to cook, tend the large vegetable garden, and help her mother with all the chores. But she took on a second job when her father Pete asked her to assist him and his friend Abdullah with their whiskey-making factory in the basement.

The details of what happened that fateful day are murky. It depends on who tells the story. There was my mom's account, her siblings' version, and her parents' somewhat sketchy interpretation. No one really knows the truth.

This is the version I remember from my mom. Though Angie was a kid, my grandfather often had her taste the finished product as it was being made. On one particularly hot day in August, as she was climbing the stairs from the basement, she became dizzy from the taste of the moonshine and overcome by the heat and fumes. She tried to regain her balance but fell down the stairs. At the bottom was a large cauldron of boiling corn mash. As she got up, still reeling, she stumbled backward into the enormous boiling pot.

Fast forward to Good Samaritan Hospital in Zanesville, where a young girl was fighting for her life. Severe burns covered the majority of her backside. The doctors decided the only way to save her was to perform skin grafts. In an innovative and painful procedure, the surgeons harvested skin from her oldest brother, Dominic, and grafted it onto her backside. He was conscious during the entire procedure and though he came out of it with scars on his back, he helped save his sister. It was a sacrifice Angie acknowledged by naming the second Missimi son Dominic (me) after her brother.

While the incident was horrific, Angie's two-year recovery resulted in a lifetime of stories about her tragic tale. My mom had the ability to turn this horrible accident into something quite amusing, especially in her colorful retelling. She loved to recount the story and end with "Look! I lost half my ass!" She loved the stories of trips to the dress shops to find garments that would not highlight her missing buttock. "I need a little more fullness in the back, please," she'd say to the salesperson—placing the woman's hand on her missing butt cheek—"you see, I had a terrible accident!" Of course the salesgirl's mouth would drop open and she would stand there speechless. Even when I brought home college friends and signaled my mom with copious gestures for her *not* to tell the story, she'd launch into yet another, embroidered retelling of her sad but juicy tale.

This was one of the first incidents that proved the desperation of my parents and grandparents to make a living for their family in their new country. Earning money was the only solution to raising a family in America. My parents taught themselves everything—how to start and run a small trucking company with a man, my father, who worked as many hours as he could withstand, and a woman, my mother, who was there by his side running the business. I still am amazed at exactly how they found the money to send me to college, but they did. I never wanted for anything when I was young. I had all the things the rich kids from the other side of the tracks had, because my dad was willing to break his back to give them to me.

My mother used to say it best. "If you work your ass off, you'll get your reward." She always paused after that line and added with a smile, "Of course, I only had to work half as hard!"

A MASS TO REMEMBER

In elementary school, church was a daily event. Everyone arrived at 7:30 and we put our book bags in our desks and our lunch sacks in the box at the rear of the classroom. By 7:45 Sister Lea, our first-grade teacher, was instructing us: “All right children, we’re ready to go to Mass. All girls, put on your chapel veils and all boys, button up your shirts and comb your hair. You are going into the house of the Lord and you must look your best!”

I loved Sister Lea. She was tiny, less than five feet tall, and without a doubt the kindest and most motherly woman I knew, next to my mom. I always have this image of her standing in the hallway of the boy’s bathroom. We had to pass her on our way to the urinals. But she stood there, like a devout bobble-head figure, hands folded in the classic “prayer” pose. “Remember boys, even the lavatory is a place of God.”

Nicky, top row left

Monday through Friday, without fail, we marched in two lines—boys in one and girls in the other—over to the church a short distance from the school. While I always was assigned to serve Mass on Sundays and special occasions like weddings and funerals, I seldom had to serve a school Mass and, in first grade, I was too young. By the time I got to sixth grade, though, I began to take seriously my serving duties. My buddies and I regularly tested the possibility of excommunication by sneaking altar wine and eating large handfuls of unconsecrated hosts. We loved reporting back to our friends about our daring doings in the sacristy.

But one day something extraordinary and frightening happened. I'm sure it has been permanently imprinted in the minds of all my classmates. I was sitting in a pew next to my buddy John Harrison, and we were desperately trying to get my cousin Mary to turn around and whisper to us. In the midst of our attempts, we heard the main door of the church burst open behind us, hitting the wall with an enormous thud. We remained looking forward because we knew if we turned around, every nun in the church would begin working her little clicker—"cut it out; turn around and obey!" While Sister Lea was a tiny woman, she possessed the loudest clicker in the school. One click could stop you dead in your tracks.

What was going on?

We were trying to look sideways to catch a glimpse of the late intruder. Mass had not begun and our parish priest, Father Donovan, was nowhere to be seen. Who was coming down the aisle?

Holy cow! I thought. It's Maxine, a woman who lived in our neighborhood and had quite a reputation. I'd often heard my mom call her a drunk. She had told me dozens of times to stay away from Maxine. "She's trouble. She's dangerous, honey. Always drinkin' and doesn't really know what she's doing. You gotta feel sorry for her, but stay away from her, you hear?"

I kept sneaking a look. Maxine was wearing a wrinkly cotton dress and a raggedy sweater. Her hair was frizzy and red; it looked like she had dyed it recently but had not done a good job. More interesting than her clothes and her disheveled hair, however, was what she held in her arms—a baby, maybe a few months old.

I think his name was Joey. That's what my mom told me when Maxine had him. The baby didn't cry, but gazed around the church and stared at the wide-eyed children staring back at him.

Maxine walked slowly up the aisle, almost like a bride, with that strange, halting step. Step, touch, step, touch, step, touch. We knew something was going to happen and we were quite certain it was going to be something bad. It didn't take more than a minute before we were proved right.

She held the baby with one arm as she began to ascend the stairs leading to the altar. She stayed centered on the carpet runner as if she had been directed to be there for the best possible effect. If she was drunk it didn't show because she took each step with grace and perfect balance as she carried her baby.

She seemed to be surveying the space—looking at each of the statues surrounding the altar. Saint Joseph was on one side and the church's namesake, Saint Rose of Lima, on the other, holding a crucifix and wearing a crown of roses. High on a pedestal overlooking the congregation stood the Blessed Mother in her mantle of blue. Slowly Maxine looked up to the stained-glass window that backed the main altar. She seemed to be in a trance as she gazed at the slender, multi-colored depiction of the Sacred Heart, with Jesus's flaming heart. She stood frozen, as still as the statues.

I grabbed John's arm. "What's she doing?" I whispered, making sure Sister Lea did not hear me. John just shrugged his shoulders in that how-am-I-supposed-to-know gesture.

Maxine gently lifted her baby and set his back against the tabernacle. I think she wanted him to be perfectly positioned but he slid slightly to the side. The baby was calm. In fact, he smiled, as if happy to see a church full of children paying attention to him.

In a quick gesture Maxine pulled a pacifier from her dress pocket and put it in the baby's mouth. He sucked fiercely. It was the only sound in a church that was holding its breath.

Slowly she turned to face us. After a second she opened her mouth to speak, but nothing came out. Then it did, and her voice overwhelmed the church.

"This is Jesus Christ!" she proclaimed. And she did proclaim it. Like she was a prophet or a famous actor or Billy Graham. "This is Jesus Christ," she repeated, "and I want you all to adore Him! He is the Son of God!" She was pointing to little Joey, but he was just sucking on his binky, oblivious to his new name.

We were 200 students from Saint Rose of Lima Elementary School, sitting in Saint Rose of Lima Church, catatonic. What to do? No one moved or said a word.

Finally, the meekest of them all, our tiny Sister Lea, bravely approached the altar as if marching to her doom. Just as she reached the steps, Father Donovan came to her rescue. He walked swiftly from the sacristy with arms outstretched, suggesting he was there to help the woman. He put his arms around her and spoke very softly so no one could hear what was being said. Sister Lea scooped the baby into her arms, as if to protect him from the sacrilege that had just occurred. She rocked him gently and the baby seemed to enjoy the attention, even making a few coos of contentment. Father Donovan nodded to Sister Lea and Maxine and pointed to the sacristy. The frightened nun, the slurping child, the dazed woman, and the astonished priest slowly made their exit.

Sister Rosalie, the school principal, came to the front of the church and directed us to return to school. "We will not have Mass today," she said. That was an understatement! After witnessing the reincarnation of Jesus Christ, I was certain that we didn't need a boring Mass.

I never heard much about Maxine after that remarkable five minutes. I believe she moved away or perhaps was sent away to "dry out."

Several years later, one of my mom's friends who lived near us on Monument Square paid a visit, accompanied by a cute, well-mannered little boy. She said "Nicky, have you ever met my nephew Joey?"

"No, I don't think I have," I said, with as much veracity as I could muster. Yes, I thought to myself. I have met him. The last time I met him he was leaning against the tabernacle at Saint Rose of Lima Church, sucking on a pacifier. I believe his mother told me his name was Jesus.

FUZZY

No dogs! Those were the rules handed to me from early childhood. My parents were not so offended by the presence of cats, as long as they never came in the house. Our neighborhood was home to a number of feral cats. You couldn't touch them or pick them up to hold them. My parents thought it was fine to let the cats wander in and out of our basement via a torn screen in a cellar window. When I saw a large tabby cat exiting the basement with a dead rat in its mouth, I understood why they had no objection to our visiting felines.

When my newlywed sister Regina and her groom Ralphie moved into the house my father built for them, the first present the young couple gave each other was a dog. It was a mix of collie and something else; I didn't know dog breeds back then. He had a warm brown coat with cream-colored streaks. I visited my new friend daily, changing his water, walking him around the neighborhood, and teaching him the standard tricks. For some reason they named him Fuzzy, though it didn't seem to have anything to do with the dog. But I didn't care. He was my new best friend.

During the long winter months, I felt so bad for him. He howled and barked incessantly, perhaps from the freezing cold that penetrated his wooden doghouse behind the shrine of Saint Theresa. Often his pie-pan of kitchen leftovers seemed to contain as many ice crystals as scraps and his water bowl was frozen solid. I often asked if I could warm him up indoors, but the answer always was "No! No dogs in the house!"

None of the Italian kids in my neighborhood had pet dogs. As I grew older, I sometimes thought it was because of what their families had endured during World War II. Perhaps they had to resort to eating dogs as food, just like the many horses that were slaughtered for human consumption. I actually ate some *cavallo* (horse) on my last trip to Sicily. While it wasn't served in my cousins' homes, it was on the menu in a small family trattoria. It wasn't horrible, but I did gag—perhaps more than was necessary—before I put the first tiny morsel in my mouth. Always a touch of the theatrical for me!

And so we grew together. A boy and "their" dog, but I came to think of him as my own and my sister was thrilled that she had a new helper with her frisky pup.

A number of farms skirted the town and I liked trapesing across their fields, lobbing pieces of fallen corn stalks and watching Fuzzy retrieve them. One of my favorite early-spring activities was flying kites. I'd buy a 15-cent paper kite from Wade Kimball's Jack Sprat Valley Market in addition to a Clark bar for my reward once I got the kite in the air. It took only 15 minutes for me to get to the enormous field of the McGonagle farm and settle on the gently sloping hill leading up to the farmhouse and barn. I loved the challenge of getting my kite to take to the air. Time after time I ran up the hill clutching it in hopes that the paper diamond would catch the wind and begin its ascent into the wide expanse of blue. Finally, I got it high off the ground and was able to hold the string gently as I sat down and took out my Clark bar. I deserved it. I had taken only a bite when the sudden "pow" of a gunshot echoed behind me. Then there was a second shot. What was happening? Where's my dog?

I looked up at the kite. It was dancing back and forth and seemed tempted to turn a somersault. I couldn't worry about the kite. I let go of the string and only watched momentarily as the kite rose higher and began to panic in its freedom. I turned toward the farmhouse.

"Fuzzy!" I yelled as loud as I could. "Fuzzy, where are you?" I was running breathlessly toward the fence that surrounded the farmhouse. People had warned us kids to stay clear of Old Man McGonagle's farm. Though he lived in a dilapidated farmhouse he was not a farmer—just a crotchety old loner who had a reputation for being a bit "touched." As I reached the fence gate I noticed the signs that hung from the broken-down enclosure.

PRIVATE PROPERTY KEEP OUT

Just inside the fence I could see the chicken coop and several scrawny hens scratching at the feed scattered on the ground. And there, lying at the entrance to the enclosure, was Fuzzy, whimpering and licking his leg, where blood was oozing out of a wound. I let out a squeal and ran to him. But a raspy voice shut me up instantly.

"Get your goddam dog off my property! He was in my hen house!"

I turned to look and standing in the doorway was Old Man McGonagle, dressed in dirty bib overalls, a tattered denim jacket, and a slouchy hat that almost covered his face. What I could see of his face was frightening. He had small, piercing eyes, a face of stubble, and an Abraham Lincoln nose. He was holding a shotgun.

"Get that mutt off my property before I call the police and have you arrested for trespassing! That son of a bitch killed one of my chickens!"

I was petrified, afraid he would turn the gun on me after shooting poor Fuzzy. I ran to the dog and saw that his leg was bleeding badly. Just beyond Fuzzy I could see one of the chickens lying in the mud. As best as I could, I put my arms around Fuzzy and tried to lift him up gently, but he was fighting me, panicked from the pain and confusion. He was almost as big as I was, and I tried desperately to readjust my hold on him. Mr. McGonagle was getting impatient and took a few steps toward me. I knew if it was anyone but me trying to pick him up, Fuzzy would have snapped and perhaps taken a bite. But he trusted me. I finally hoisted him high enough that I could squeeze him close to my body yet keep his bleeding leg away from me.

As quickly as I could, I began to run down the hill. I tried talking to Fuzzy to put him at ease. "It's okay, boy, you're gonna be fine! I'll get you home and we'll fix you up. You'll see. You're gonna be fine." By the time I was walking past my backpack and the wrapper from my Clark bar that lay in the grass, I was bawling my eyes out. "You're gonna be okay, Fuz. You're gonna be okay!"

Of course I wasn't sure he was going to be okay. What if he died in my arms? His whimpering subsided and I was afraid he was giving up. I ordered my feet to move, even though the weight of the dog was beginning to drag me down.

An eternity later, I arrived at Regina's house and after screaming her name over and over, she ran out and made way for me to bring Fuzzy into the laundry room.

Within a few minutes Regina had contacted Ralphie and Fuzzy was whisked away to the vet, who fixed him up and sent him home with a splint on his leg. I had bowls of dog food and fresh water waiting for him when he hobbled into the laundry room. "Hey buddy! Look at you! You're all better!" He licked my face again and again and seemed to not want to stop thanking me for bringing him home.

For several years following the shooting, when July rolled around, Fuzzy instinctively took cover. Around July 1st he'd begin to find secret hideouts to protect against the sounds of firecrackers and cherry bombs. He seemed to know he would have to live through hundreds of "gunshots" when the neighborhood boys began their Fourth of July celebrations. For Fuzzy, it was his least favorite day of the year. We wouldn't get near him for the entire day. But on July 5th, we always made sure he had special treats and a day filled with hugs and an unending stack of sticks to fetch. And we talked very softly. Even the normally loud Regina.

CHERRY TREES AND MEATBALLS

Each summer brought one week of total enjoyment for my cousin Mary and me. It was the Missimi family vacation, the modest and inexpensive car trip to northern Ohio to visit my dad's parents, several other Italian families, and the big highlight—a trip to Cedar Point amusement park in Sandusky (above).

It was only a four-hour drive to Bellevue, where Grandpa Tony and Grandma Maria lived on Railroad Street. Getting there was like sitting in the middle of a produce truck—with Mary and I in the back seat, buried under baskets of tomatoes, peppers, cucumbers, cantaloupes, baked goods, and Mason jars of canned peaches. These were the gifts from our garden and mom's cellar.

"You can't show up empty-handed," mom said. "You have to bring nice things for the people who are going to put you up for a week."

My *nonni* (grandparents) lived in a small wooden house just a few feet away from the tracks of the Nickel Plate Railroad. The house had no indoor plumbing, so the most memorable aspect of our temporary home was the horrible outhouse—a toilet seat on a wooden bench and a toilet paper holder nailed to the wall. We had to be forced to pay a visit to the little wooden structure, but only if an adult stood watch near the door, "in case a snake bit our bottoms."

Every morning I watched Grandpa Antonio (Tony) gather eggs from his hen house, tap a large brown egg with a spoon, and suck down its contents. I remember Grandma Maria sitting on a three-legged stool, scalding a chicken in a pot of boiling water as she plucked its feathers. She had wrung its neck just a few minutes before. Many afternoons Mary and I were bathed in a large, galvanized tub in the ghostly cave they called the basement. We filled the tub with the garden hose and grandma brought several buckets of hot water down from the kitchen. We never were embarrassed, though we made sure we didn't face each other when we had to stand up to have my mom give us a good scrub.

Our favorite spot was the shiny-skinned cherry tree in the back yard. We loved climbing its branches and eating the sweet fruit as we scrambled up to our lookout perch at the top. Two limbs connected to create a perfect throne where Mary and I could survey our family's kingdom. We were happiest sitting on top of our world, giggling at the frantic behavior of the Italian relatives slamming in and out of the screened door below.

Even though summertime was not for studying, on this vacation I learned an important lesson about meatballs. Because there were many children in the houses we visited, the mammas thought it was essential to satisfy the children by serving them pasta and meatballs at all our family dinners.

We ate at a different house at least five of the seven nights. I discovered that Mrs. Mira's meatballs were ridiculously small—the size of the largest marbles in my prized collection of glass beauties. Mrs. Incovia's were like small, circular meatloaves, much too big to be called a meatball. Aunt Linda's were perfectly sized and so tender that they fell apart at the touch of a fork. Aunt Catherine's were a delicious mix filled with *parmigiano* and lots of garlic. But Grandma Maria's were my hands-down favorite. They were perfect in every way, just the size and taste that a meatball should be, and just like the ones my mom made for every Sunday pasta dinner.

The highlight of our trip every summer was a visit to Cedar Point for a day of fun and frolicking at the famous amusement park on the shores of Lake Erie.

For several years Mary and I had to be content with the kid's rides—the merry-go-round, the gigantic silver rocket ride, and the swings. But we couldn't go on what we thought must be the best ride—the wooden roller coaster. This required that we measure up to the correct height on an over-sized ruler on display at its entrance. So Mary and I could only watch and dream about what it would be like to experience the terrifying speed and rattling, clackety noise of the wooden coaster that dipped so dangerously close to the lake.

Once we'd exhausted ourselves with a morning of rides and cotton candy, we headed toward the beach where mom and dad and my relatives waited with an Italian picnic lunch in the shadow of the elegant Breakers Hotel. It was typical—a hunk of provolone cheese, salami you sliced with a knife, homemade Italian bread, fried green and red peppers, and sliced tomatoes. In my estimation, the perfect lunch—the one I shared with my parents most days during the hot summer months.

For our return to New Lex, Mary and I again were squished into the back seat, sandwiched between new baskets of tomatoes, peppers, melons, green beans, and zucchini from Grandpa Tony's garden. Best of all, we rode home with baskets of ruby red cherries on our laps and a paper cup to spit out the pits. It was the perfect finale to our wonderful *vacanza Italiana!*

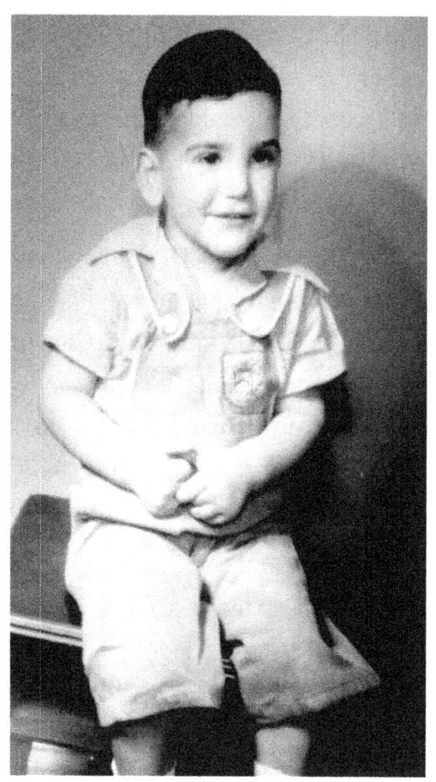

THE BOYHOOD OF NICKY

For the 18 years I lived in the house at 714 North Main, I was Nicky, though I certainly preferred to be called Nick. Only when I left for college in Detroit in 1962 did people begin to call me Dominic. I liked both my names, just not "Nicky." That's what you called the nerdy kid who posed for his fourth-grade photo in his too-tight flannel shirt, shiny corduroy trousers, and Hopalong Cassidy cowboy belt. "Nicky" is not a name for the dark-skinned Italian-American teenager I would grow up to be. As a young boy, though, I always smiled when my grandma called me "Nicootz," a term of endearment for her chubby little grandson.

Once I arrived at the University of Detroit, my boyhood home on North Main began to fade away along with "Nicky." It was now the place I came home to for Thanksgiving, Christmas, and Easter to stuff my face with Angie's remarkable *cucina Italiana.* But following graduation from college, I moved into my own apartment and trips back to New Lex were sporadic—definitely at Christmas and, sadly, a series of funerals for aunts and uncles and most painfully, my mom and dad.

It's interesting to stand back and observe myself as a young boy. Physically I carried a little more weight than most of my friends. I wasn't fat, but I wasn't pleased when my mother took me to Penney's to buy back-to-school pants in the boys' "husky" section. High school was similar. My friends were slim with flat stomachs, well-developed pecs, and muscular bodies, while I was plagued with my constantly growing man-boobs. My friend Butchy Epifano, who had a similar problem, loved to tease me. "When are you getting your training bra, Nicky?" My buddies were the running backs on the football team while I moved from center position to guard and then finally to tackle—big-guy positions. I weighed 180 and was 5'11" with a 36-inch waist. Snapshots show that I carried myself well, because I never appeared overweight, just "biggish," and even a little "brawny." I liked the looks of my rock-star idols, like Elvis, and dressed in the requisite jeans and white tee shirt. But I also liked the well-scrubbed look of Pat Boone and Ricky Nelson and all the Italian-American pop stars—Frankie Avalon and Fabian were at the top of my list.

Each year of elementary school had a certain rhythm, filled with daily and seasonal routines. School-day breakfasts were toast and hot chocolate or, some mornings, "sapooch" made by Grandma Victoria. Lunches were baloney sandwiches with mustard or peanut butter and jelly and a carton of chocolate milk from the dairy next to the school. There was the full day of classes at Saint Rose of Lima Elementary School, mostly taught by the Sisters of Saint Francis of Penance and Christian Charity, and eventually football practice once I arrived in sixth grade.

From the time I was a small child, my cousin Mary was my best friend and we spent much of our time together. Every morning we walked up the "straight hill" to school and descended the same hill at the end of the day. We did everything together, from creating a carnival in the back yard with toys and empty cardboard boxes and refuse from the tire company next door, to raking leaves from the massive sycamore tree in front of 714 North Main into a large heap. In the 1950s it was still okay to burn leaves on your property. We danced around the booming bonfire as my dad raked leaves into an ever-growing mountain of flames. I always was thrilled to see the leaves turn in September. I knew there'd be bonfires by Halloween.

Summers, however, were the joy of my existence as a kid. It meant a season pass at the municipal swimming pool and three months of unending bike rides with my buddies. I could travel to any part of our small town in a matter of minutes. Summer also meant no shoes whenever possible. But "no shoes" also brought back memories of my mom scrubbing the bottoms of my feet with gasoline to remove the tar. The alley next to our house led to the Ready-Mix Cement Company and it was paved with blacktop. In the summer heat, the blacktop oozed, and I remember dancing gingerly down the road to get into our back yard. "Don't you dare put those goddam feet on my clean white sheets!" screamed my mom.

Though I was not a true sportsman, I played sports out of necessity. It's what every other all-American kid was supposed to do, so I joined the teams, including Little League. I was left-handed so I gravitated to the first-base position, and a brand-new Ted Kluszewski (Cincinnati Reds) mitt made me feel like the poster child for a well-dressed Little Leaguer. Even at that age I appreciated the costume more than the game. I always made sure my uniform was carefully ironed and immaculate, secretly hoping my fine appearance would make up for the fact that I was a mediocre player.

For a brief moment in the summer of 1955, though, I became a star. I played for the Jets, my Little League team. I was at the plate. Hitting was my worst attribute as a ball player. I was fast and could catch, but I couldn't hit worth a damn.

But on this day, I was anointed. The pitch came at me and as it rolled from Johnny Burns' hand, it roared straight as an arrow toward home plate. It seemed a perfect pitch. I lifted my chest and lifted the bat a little higher, too. My right foot stepped forward and with all my might, I laid into the ball. There was an astounding crack when the bat made contact, and I stood stock-still in amazement as the ball sailed high into the air. It soared over the field—clearing the fence, floating above the flagpole, and continuing its journey into the back yard of a neighbor hundreds of feet away.

As I slowly circled the bases, slapping hands with my teammates, I had only one thought: Coach is gonna buy me anything I want at the Dairy Freeze after the game! And so he did. I chose a banana split with chocolate, marshmallow, and strawberry toppings as my reward for one of the longest home runs in New Lex Little League history.

Mine was a relatively simple childhood with a number of standout events, including partnering with my cousin Mary as a miniature bride and groom for my sister Regina's wedding. There was my First Holy Communion. There were countless family gatherings with the Italian relatives. There were the mouth-dropping and mouth-watering holiday feasts prepared by my mom (with 50 pies at Christmas!). And there was the constant stream of house guests sitting under the arbor for a summer's evening of hospitality by Angie.

During many of these family gatherings I played the smiling waiter, carrying hot coffee, glasses of wine, or bottles of orange soda on a beautifully painted Sicilian tray. It was hard to keep everything balanced, though, while under attack by well-meaning relatives and neighbors who wanted to pinch my cheeks or ruffle my hair or slap my butt.

They also wanted to talk about me. Balancing her coffee on her knee, Annie DiBari often spoke over the other guests' conversation. "Oh, *comare*, look how big your Nicky is getting!" I'd be sitting in the middle of all these Italians, drinking my orange pop and devouring large quantities of Italian cookies. I loved them all, except the biscotti with the anise flavor. (Now, however, they are among my favorites.) And I never missed the Nicky compliments that flew over my head.

"*Si, comare*, but he'll always be my little boy!" said my mom.

"Nicootz" was the kid.

"Nicky" was the little boy.

"Dominic Eugene!" was my mom's warning.

"Dominic" was the college student and teacher.

"Dom" was the friend.

And "Domenico" was the Italian boy with a sense of the theatrical.

I answered to all my names and loved them all.

THE SHACK IN THE BACK

Our closest neighbors were two strange women who lived in a shanty just beyond the 50-gallon oil drum where we burned our trash. They easily could have been created by Carson McCullers in one of her Southern Gothic novels. They were as much "local color" as one could imagine in my small, run-of-the-mill town. While there were other citizens in coal-mining New Lex who were high on my list of strange inhabitants, these two women were the most memorable.

Mary Blackburn and Dixie Carter. They lived in an almost uninhabitable shack, a small, two-room structure made of wood, but one that had never felt the kiss of a paint brush. Since most of the wood siding had rotted, the building was black and foreboding. It was one story, with rough cement floors and a pot-bellied stove in the middle of the room, its coal-black pipe running up to the smokestack. A concrete front porch was level with the alley in front of the house. The alley was the same pot-holed, blacktop roadway (Mechanic Street) that went by the side of my house. It was used mainly by the trucks that kicked up dust and stones as they barreled along, racing to fill their spinning drums with a new load of Ready-Mix concrete.

These two women were the personification of strange. Mary Blackburn seemed to be old, perhaps in her 70s, but when you looked at her face, you weren't sure. It was almost the face of a child. Her skin was smooth and her eyes twinkled, but her body was small and fragile and she hobbled around her tiny world like a gnome. The only skin you could see was her face—otherwise she was clothed from neck to ankles in dark pioneer dresses, with equally somber aprons. These may well have been her sleeping clothes. She had no teeth that I could see, and her lips curled into her mouth like the facial contortions we made when we were trying to imitate a witch. When she spoke—and she was a woman of very few words—she whispered, as if she were incapable of speaking with any resonance. She rarely made a statement, though, only commenting on other people's statements. "Mmmmm" was her most common response, with her head bobbing up and down if she agreed or "mmmmm" with her head moving left to right if she didn't. She mainly sat on her dirt-smeared wooden rocker, her mouth constantly moving, not with words, but with tobacco. She liked a good chaw.

Her friend Dixie was the town's strangest citizen. I had no idea what their relationship was. I presumed Dixie was some kind of caretaker, since she was at least 20 years younger than Old Mary Blackburn. She was tall and always dressed in men's clothing. She wore her trousers very high, riding just under her bosom, so she had the look of a sad-sack comedian, perhaps from some Middle-European circus. But when she opened her mouth to speak, it was clear she was from the South, with an almost impenetrable drawl that made each word last twice as long as normal. Her hair was short and resembled a fright wig, obviously cut by herself or Mary. It was a dark brown tangle, like an unruly Afro, though Dixie was not black. In fact, her face was unusually white, and she always wore a straw cowboy hat to keep the sun from reaching her creamy, albino-like skin. She wore cowboy boots with hard wooden heels that clacked as she walked down the alley, occasionally crossing over a crumbling piece of blacktop like a flamenco dancer.

She passed by the gate to our back yard several times a day, returning from her walks around town. Often I'd be playing with Fuzzy, or washing dad's Pontiac, or sweeping up grapes that had fallen from the arbor when her voice would get my attention.

"Howdy, Nicky," she drawled.

"Good morning, Dixie. How's Old Mary Blackburn?" I always called her "Old Mary Blackburn." Even when I spoke to the ancient pioneer woman herself, I'd say, "How you been, Old Mary Blackburn?"

"She doin' jus fine, Nicky," Dixie said, never making eye contact as she continued her saunter down the road. "She'll be happy I got her some Mail Pouch."

Dixie often crossed North Main to go to the Jack Sprat Valley Market. Seldom for food, but mainly for chewing tobacco and Clark bars or a few meat scraps from Mr. Kimball's dodgy meat case. If Old Mary Blackburn had any teeth, they wouldn't last long with all the candy she consumed.

Although Dixie spent nickels and dimes on tobacco and candy bars, when it came to nourishing food she relied on handouts. Over the fence she'd say, "You got a can of pork'n beans for me and Ole Mary, Nicky?" This was a regular occurrence.

"I think I can find you one, Dixie." And I always did, just as I would find canned soups and vegetables for the Hoops brothers, two hobos who lived near the railroad tracks and often knocked on our kitchen door for a handout. They were a frightening pair—apparitions, dirty and disheveled, staring at me through the window with a pitiful look. You got anything for us, Nicky boy? their eyes said to me. But I never thought anything bad about them. Not then. Today I would call the cops.

I remember sitting on Old Mary Blackburn's tiny porch, Mary in her special chair and Dixie in a battered rocker that had lost every bit of its varnish. I sat on a large, upside-down, red clay pot that probably never had a living thing growing in it.

"Tell me about the circus, Dixie." She always loved this request.

"You wanna hear about my days with the circus? Those were some helluva good memories." With a smile on her lips, she'd take out a small, dark brown wooden pipe and light up. Everything about the house and porch had that sweet smell of tobacco, with a little hint of cherry. In the midst of the poverty and squalor, the scent was very comforting.

"I did everything for Mr. Magee, the circus owner." Dixie closed her eyes and began her journey back in time. "I fed the animals every day and had to haul their shit in buckets to a trailer we hitched to a tractor. 'Course I helped git the tent up and all the riggin' but I mostly remember I got to ride a beautiful horse for the grand finale. I didn't do no tricks or nothin.' I just sat up there on Palamina—so purdy with her beauty-full brown body and long blonde mane. She was somthun! And I looked pretty good too, in my spangly costume! 'Course I didn't wear one of those skimpy circus things. I was dressed like a cowgirl, with chaps and a fancy western shirt with brown and gold sequins and spangles hangin' down." She stood and sashayed around the porch, modeling her imaginary costume. "Jesus, lover of my soul, those were the good old days!"

She loved me bringing up the circus. It was Dixie's moment to float away while Old Mary Blackburn hummed a favorite spiritual—a strange duet with her squeaky rocker—with tobacco juice running down her chin.

I left for college when I was 18, and though for many years I returned home for the holidays I rarely walked by Old Mary

Blackburn's house. On one of my visits home, I was in the kitchen when I thought of the two of them. I went to the cupboard, took out a can of VanKamp's Pork and Beans, and headed out the door. The house was still there—totally abandoned with its windows broken, the smokestack lying on its side on the battered tin roof, and the front door missing, inviting anyone and anything to take a peek—or a pee. I walked to the door and stuck my head inside. I knew it would be ugly and desolate, but I wanted to be transported back to the days of Dixie's circus tales and me and Old Mary Blackburn listening intently. After a few seconds, a breeze carried the scent of cherry tobacco to my nose. I inhaled. I smelled it. And just as quickly, it was gone. The only thing that seemed to have survived was the upside-down red clay pot on the porch. I placed my little gift on the pot, knowing that the Hoops brothers might find it. "Enjoy the beans, guys. And goodbye, sweet ladies."

CHIARASCURO

I sometimes think my life has been painted by Caravaggio. Chiaroscuro was his trademark—a study in light and shadow, filled with the beautiful and the profane, the saint and the sinner. He was one of my favorite Renaissance painters. But for now, I want to concentrate on the light streaming through the window, illuminating me as in Caravaggio's famous painting, "The Calling of Saint Matthew" (above). No dark, mysterious shadows, just the joy of inspiring light.

In spite of being a religious zealot as a youngster, I eventually grew up to be a sometime church-going Catholic, and my "goody-two-shoes" life faded once I discovered sin in high school.

My first encounter with religious fervor was in 1950 at the age of six, when my cousin Mary and I processed down the aisle as miniature bride and groom at my sister Regina's wedding at Saint Rose of Lima Church. It was a large, over-staged Italian affair. The church was decorated with an arch of flowers at the communion rail, large white blossoms and bows on the pews, and white roses as far as the eye could see. I thought it was a glimpse of heaven. The memory of the wedding reminded me that I always have equated religious experiences with beauty and ritual. All my religious experiences have those shafts of colored light spilling through the stained-glass windows. Not surprising for a person who would choose theatre as a lifetime vocation—I always felt that lighting was the most important element in creating theatrical magic.

By the time I was in eighth grade I was head altar boy at church and was scheduled to serve regularly, particularly at Sunday Mass and all special feast days. My piety swelled whenever I was assigned to be the cross bearer at the Benediction service. The congregation sat in a smoky haze of incense as my best friend George swung the thurible, sending streams of the spicy, sandalwood fragrance to permeate the nave. The choir sang "*Pange lingua gloriosi.*" More high drama and I had tears in my eyes. I felt very close to God when I was clutching my cross and reciting my Latin responses better than any of my friends. I was in a play. I was one of God's little actors and I loved my part!

Throughout elementary school I had a special devotion to the Blessed Virgin Mary. Perhaps I was inspired by my mom's constant praying of the rosary and regular attendance at novenas. Each year I put together a May altar in my bedroom, since May was the month of Mary. It seemed appropriate—especially in a room that was as much a chapel as a bedroom. Against one wall was my brother Tony's *prie-deux*, a kneeler he used when he was home from the seminary. Several religious pictures adorned the walls along with a traditional crucifix above my bed, the kind that contained candles and holy oil in case a priest needed to administer the sacrament of Extreme Unction, the last rites. On one of the side tables beside my bed sat a large, dog-eared volume of *The Lives of the Saints*, my favorite bedtime reading.

I was obsessed with *The Lives of the Saints*. Actually, I was more obsessed with the deaths of the saints. Of course, I was moved by their bravery and their absolute devotion to and love of God, but I also had a rather prurient interest in their deaths. I loved to dwell on the story of the death of Saint Lawrence being grilled in a large frying pan—"Turn me over; I'm done on this side." There was Saint Bartholomew, who was skinned alive, and Saint Agatha of Sicily, whose torture included having her breasts torn from her body (as a result, she now is the patron saint of breast cancer). All hideous and gruesome deaths and yet these men and women would not give up their faith, they would not renounce their Christianity. I wanted to be just like them. I wanted to be just as brave in the face of torture and death.

I remember a little nun, Sister Thomas, asking my fourth-grade classmates, "And what will you do when the Communists come to our school and line you up against the blackboard and point their machine guns at you?"

What would I do? I thought. Would I be brave like Saint Peter, and let them crucify me upside down? I remember when she looked right at me. "And what would you do, Dominic?"

I knew what she wanted me to say. "I will not give up my faith," I said. "I am a Catholic."

The good sisters did a fine job of making me a proud and devout Catholic. I rushed to the confessional if I forgot and ate a baloney sandwich on Friday. I sat in embarrassment while everyone stood to receive the Holy Eucharist because I had a blood-rushing impure thought during the Epistle. Plus, I was sitting in the pew with an erection. Oh my God! Two mortal sins in a matter of minutes. If a car ran over me as I left the church, I'd be damned to hell for eternity!

I spent many of my adolescent years wandering through the garden of mortal sins. I figured I was like every other boy my age. Sometimes I wandered a little deeper into the garden, where there were shadows lurking in the corners. But I always seemed to find my light. After all, I was an actor. I knew how to locate the hot spots on my stage.

THE 20-KISS WIENER ROAST

It was a perfect autumn night for a wiener roast. Pam Mace, who lived halfway up the "straight hill," about seven houses from my house on North Main, had invited all of the seventh-grade class for a Halloween wiener roast.

The party was held around a gigantic bonfire built in the enormous expanse of her back yard. The property sloped down to a cornfield, with some open pasture where a few work horses grazed in the evening light. They were enormous beasts, much larger than race horses and almost essential for farm work.

All my friends from the eighth grade were there also—my best friend George Sagan and several other guys I liked to hang out with.

After playing a steady hit-parade medley of the most popular 45s—Brenda Lee, Johnny Mathis, The Platters—we finally got around to the wieners, sometimes roasting two at a time, showing off our gargantuan appetites and our skill with our hand-carved roasting sticks.

Stuffed with the bonfired supper, many of us wandered down to the fence that separated the yard from the harvested cornfield. Butchy Epifano was on the other side, herding the horses toward our group at the fence. I was leaning near the fence post, talking to beautiful Mary Lee Nash, the most popular girl in our class.

But Butchy was up to no good. Planning to torment the largest of the horses, Butchy picked up a corn cob from the field and aimed it toward the horse's anus. Just as I was contemplating putting my arm around Mary Lee's shoulders, the enormous, black-maned horse reared its head over the fence, bit into my back, picked me up off the ground, and flipped me over the fence, landing at its feet. As I looked up into the horse's eyes, Butchy slapped its rump to shoo it away, as if to get rid of the evidence. The girls were screaming and the boys did what they could to scare the other horses back up into the field.

I looked back at Mary Lee. “Oh My God, Nicky, are you all right?” she yelled from the other side of the fence.

“Yeah, I’m fine. What just happened?”

“That horse bit you and threw you over the fence,” said my buddy George. “Come on, climb back over.” George helped me get over the wood and wire fencing as a crowd assembled around me.

“Let’s see what he did,” yelled Butchy as he spun me around so everyone could get a view of my back. George lifted my shirt to the gasps and screams of the wiener-roasters. “Jesus H. Christ! Will you look at that!” yelled Butchy, almost proud of his handiwork.

“Oh my God, Nicky, you can see every one of its teeth in your back!” cried Mary Lee.

“It’s totally black and blue!” said George.

“Are you going to get lockjaw?” asked Butchy. I wanted to smash him in the face.

As the autumn moon rose, everyone returned to the bonfire for a series of kissing games. I realized then that I was grateful to Butchy. (Actually, his name was Dominic, just like mine, just like his dad’s, and just like my uncle for whom I was named.) Even Spin the Bottle kept favoring the boy with the horse bite, and every girl wanted a kiss. I never thought I’d say it: thank you, Butchy, for your attempted animal abuse. You gave me the most memorable night of junior high. Except maybe for the night my mumps fell into my testicles and I had to be hospitalized. That was memorable. But that’s another story.

HERO

I learned that I loved my dad under the worst of circumstances. We were at the Six Mile Turn Drive-In movie on the outskirts of town. My cousin Mary was with us. The drive-in had an enormous refreshment stand. Not that we were allowed to buy anything since we packed our own sacks of popcorn, a gallon thermos of orange Kool-Aid, and a couple of Snickers. But if we behaved, dad would let us get a hot dog at the flashy food stand. "Twenty-five cents for a hot dog?" My mom was shocked at the prices. "For a lousy damn wiener and a squishy bun?"

Dad always picked a cowboy movie, especially if it was with John Wayne or any of the other famous 1950s Western heroes. Mary and I sat way up front on the enormous bench at the base of the screen, a favorite spot for kids who didn't want to be cooped up in the car with their parents, constantly shushing them to be quiet.

We were barely settled when we heard the sound of tires screeching on the asphalt and the cacophony of crashing metal and breaking glass. In a matter of seconds an enormous cloud of smoke rose up behind the screen. It was clear to everyone that an accident had just happened at the entrance to the drive-in. From what we heard, we were certain it was the sound of death.

As if on cue, everyone piled out of their cars and ran to the road. We went back to our car to be with mom, but as we approached the old Pontiac dad passed us at a full trot. Mom was right behind him and we joined hands with her as we ran with everyone, hoping against hope it would not be as bad as it sounded.

But it was. Six cars were strewn across the road and on the berm. Two were on fire and several bodies were on the pavement. Some were moving and crying out in pain and others lay still, legs and arms twisted and faces smashed from the impact. Mom was horrified that we were looking at the carnage. She pulled our heads into her to help cover our eyes. We heard sirens approaching. Through the haze of smoke and fire I tried to find my dad. Where did he go? "Do you see him anywhere, Mom?"

"No, honey, I don't see him nowhere."

I stared at an accordion-crushed car, obviously the result of a head-on collision. Smoke was rising from the engine and the smell of fire and gasoline was overpowering. Through the smoke, I saw my dad. He was crawling out of the back seat of the crushed car, holding something. I gasped when I realized it was a baby, wrapped in a blanket.

"Oh my God!" my mother screamed. She lurched toward the road but Mary and I held her back.

"No, Mom!" I screamed. "Someone will help him."

No sooner had I said those words than dad was crossing to a fire engine. The fireman sent him further down the road where an ambulance had just arrived. We watched him hand the baby to one of the emergency squad. He did it so delicately, so gently, as if not to disturb the sleeping baby. We ran behind the crowd so we could be close to my dad. He caught sight of us and moved in our direction. "Let's go," he said sharply. None of us spoke. We knew it was time to be silent.

We got in the car and stared through the drive-in's screen with X-ray vision, imagining what was happening on the other side. I watched the back of my dad's head, waiting for a sign that he was okay. After a moment or two, his head moved and he began to sob. After another moment he turned to mom. "The baby died," he said. "It died right in my arms—a tiny little baby." And then came uncontrollable sobs.

Though I couldn't see his face I could feel his anguish. Mom scooted over on her seat to take his hand and do what she could to comfort him. Mary and I were crying. Not for the baby, though that was an enormous tragedy, but for my dad, the man who I had never heard say a tender word to anyone. That night he became human for me. It was a night I will remember all my life, the night I knew I loved my dad—my hero—with all my heart.

BLUE KNIGHT SPECIAL

I had a wonderful high school experience. While so many popular books, movies, and musicals are filled with high school angst—the trademark of most adults' memories of their disappointing and unfulfilling high school "daze"—my four years were among the happiest of my life.

Everything went perfectly for me. I was president of my class all four years, number 15 on the varsity football team (above), president of the Catholic Youth Organization and the Catholic Students Mission Crusade, and editor of the school newspaper and literary magazine. I played the lead in several plays, sang in the Glee Club, and dated a Latin bombshell who was Miss Nicaragua in the Miss Universe pageant.

I certainly wasn't the brightest in my class. That distinction belonged to Elaine Hayden. While not the valedictorian of our class, I believe she was the smartest because she knew how to combine her book-knowledge with an active social life. She wasn't one of those stuck-up "I'm smarter than you" girls, though she did live up on the hill with the other students whose families didn't have an Italian or Lebanese accent. For some reason, I always thought kids who lived in the nicer neighborhoods were smarter than kids of immigrant parents. I always knew she would be a success.

I got to know Elaine really well when she and I were sent to Notre Dame University as representatives of our Catholic Students Mission Crusade. We had been chosen to emcee the talent show in front of a packed house of 5,000 crusaders. To top it off, we danced a waltz in the talent portion and received an enormous ovation. It was the highlight of my junior year and it cemented my friendship with Elaine. She went on to get her Ph.D. at Ohio State and became a member of their administration in addition to serving on their Board of Regents.

I think Elaine and I turned out to be two of the most accomplished and successful of our tiny class of 36 students— "the mighty few of '62," as we called ourselves.

My high school success had a great deal to do with the amazing opportunities I was offered. Saint Aloysius Academy was a magnificent structure on a hill in the outskirts of New Lex. The most impressive aspect of the red brick, Gothic-inspired structure, built in 1887, was the chapel. Its steeple could be seen from miles away, rising majestically above the corn fields. Inside, the chapel featured a black and white mosaic tile floor in a swastika pattern, a German design popular long before it became the symbol of Hitler's Nazi Party. The chapel also contained magnificent woodwork on the three altars and elaborate stained-glass windows that spilled rainbow light on the exquisitely detailed wood-carved statues of the Sacred Heart, the Blessed Mother, and Saint Joseph.

But it wasn't just the chapel that made the school an unusually grand building for a group of students whose fathers were miners and farmers. The school featured an ornate auditorium, with a creamy white proscenium arch and lush, red velvet curtains. A painting studio housed dozens of easels and a music studio featured several private practice rooms with grand pianos. The "Social Room" was an elegant salon with a combination of Victorian, Tudor, and Elizabethan furniture. It provided a museum-like atmosphere for the school's special events. We were intimidated to enter into its grandness. All this for an enrollment of 125 students!

But there's more. Included among those 125 students were the boarders—girls who lived at the Academy and came primarily from the Columbus area.

There also were out-of-state and international students, including Maria Auxiliadora Conti from Nicaragua. She was my girlfriend during junior year and my junior prom date. I always was thrilled to be seen with this gorgeous and exotic creature. Maria had bigger hair than Annette Funicello, everyone's favorite Mouseketeer, and she appeared to be much older than our classmates. I always thought her parents sent her to St. Al's hoping she might meet and marry a rich young man and become an American citizen. I had no plans to find the girl of my dreams until I finished college and got a good job. Besides, we were a family of dirt-poor immigrants.

The Academy also had a military school for boys from third through eighth grade. The cadets lived in a separate wing and, other than watching their marching and military maneuvers on the football field, we seldom saw them.

We all came together once each year for a very special event that involved the entire enrollment of the Academy and Military School. It was the annual May Crowning.

This was a public spectacle created by the German Franciscan Sisters who founded the school. The May Crowning drew townspeople to a heart-shaped lake on campus. Several shrines of saints surrounded the lake, with the largest and most elaborate housing a statue of the Blessed Virgin Mary. Spectators arrived at the May Crowning via a hillside road leading up to the Academy.

The road was lined with a stone wall containing colored glass and pieces of broken ceramics from southeastern Ohio's famous potteries, including Crooksville and Roseville, still popular with collectors today. It was the fashion to incorporate pottery shards into many masonry projects in New Lex. The Missimis had a perfect example of this type of hodgepodge stonework—our backyard shrine to Saint Theresa/Saint Anthony.

On the day of the May Crowning the road was lined with an honor guard of cadets with swords drawn while the May Queen and her court, as well as the entire student body, processed to the lakeside shrine. Once everyone was settled on the lawn, students performed an elaborate, Bacchanalian scarf dance (usually to the tune of "Waltz of the Flowers" from *The Nutcracker*) and recited set speeches (most written in the 19th century). Many of these recitations began with "Quiet, ye winds!" or other archaic prose trying to be poetry. The event seemed more pagan than Christian, but the townspeople thought it was a Catholic slice of Cecil B. DeMille. It remains my most favorite "religious" experience in high school, though it was all dressed up like a cheap date to a tacky Italian wedding. Even the May Queen, Cecilia Daniels, was decked out in her mother's bridal gown.

I was never a top student in high school. I was too busy being social. I got by with last-minute crashing for exams and quickly scribbled papers, always written the night before the due date. I spent huge amounts of time working on projects—journalism deadlines, party decorations for dances, my cashier job at the A&P grocery store, and sports. I moved between two spheres: cruising around with my cousin Mary and the school's most popular girls and hanging out with my own group of male friends who were a combination of jocks and nerds. I enjoyed my double life of being on the football team and also being the lead in the high school play—it meant I belonged to both these polar-opposite worlds.

I had little doubt, though, that I wanted someday to be involved with the theatre or, at the very least, become a theatre critic if I didn't make it as an actor. Two women were very influential in helping me along this path.

Sister Leonardine was the principal at St. Al's, but she also directed all the major stage productions. I was fortunate that she chose me for leading roles in many of them, including my senior-year performance as Simon Peter in *The Big Fisherman*. My mom was so proud of me. She invited all her *comares* (best friends) to attend the performance. What Italian woman wouldn't want to boast that she had one son in the seminary and another one playing Saint Peter, the most famous saint of all?

Sister Christina was my journalism teacher, who constantly encouraged me to write—articles, poems, short stories, plays. She pushed me to pursue all my creative instincts and was instrumental in helping me get a journalism scholarship to the University of Detroit. Outwardly, I was a smart-mouthed high schooler who loved to make fun of our teachers, especially the nuns. Inwardly, I had a lot of respect and affection for these two wonderful women who helped me become who I am.

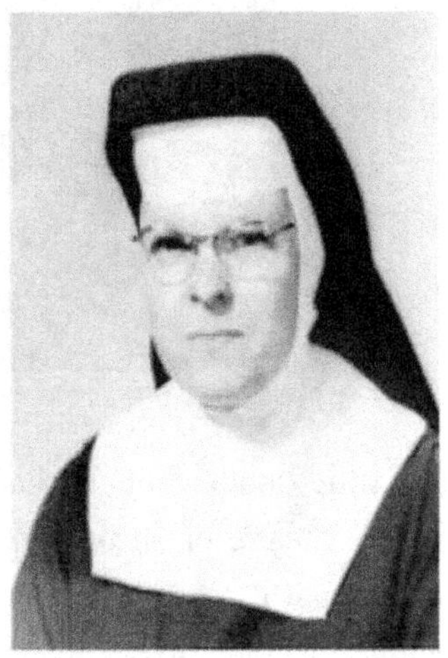

Sister Christina and Sister Leonardine

During the school year, I felt like a BMOC, with a whirlwind daily schedule that lasted from 7 a.m. to 6 p.m. But summertime was what I loved most—three months of sweet nothing—and with my first paying job, I was assured that I was going to have a "groovy" summer. The day after my 16th birthday I reported for my first day of work at the New Lexington Municipal Pool.

One of my older friends, a lifeguard, put in a good word for me with the pool manager. My job was "basket boy," handing out wire baskets that were returned to me with the swimmers' clothes once they had changed in the locker rooms. I shelved and guarded them until the swimmer was ready to leave.

The job was mindless and only demanded smiles and a sunny personality, something inherent to a southern Italian-American boy. This was the behavior my mom had coached me in for meeting our steady stream of Italian relatives. The job was more of a social occasion than work, giving me a chance to spend hours with my friends who worked as lifeguards and attendants. Just the smells of the place made me think I was on summer vacation. Every day when I walked through the turnstiles the smell of chlorinated water was like perfume and the hot dogs in the steamer and the corn popping in the refreshment stand were mouth-watering. I longed for my break so I could buy my foot-long with the works and my absolute favorite, a frozen Milky Way. That was my summer diet for 1960.

Mostly I enjoyed the privilege of diving into the pool when everyone else had to get out for rest period, a vestige of the polio scare of previous decades. I loved blowing my whistle (I also was an assistant lifeguard) to clear the pool so the guards could take to the diving boards, showing off their best dives and antic clowning. There were about 10 of us, preening and posturing in front of the pool-full of spectators on the sidelines. There I was, a slightly pudgy, dark-complexioned Italian boy, frolicking with his bronzed, super-buff friends sailing off the high board with jackknife dives and bomb-like cannon balls. Twice a day, for 10 minutes, I was part of the very "cool" sexy high school jocks. I didn't belong there, but I was proud of myself for finding a way to be part of this popular clique. Watching the spectacle of the lifeguards' aquatic escapades, I came up with an idea for the first theatrical production I would create. But more on that when I talk about my life in the theatre.

I loved hanging with my friends in the summer. I looked forward to stealing watermelons from the A&P (they left them outside the store in large bins), going to the drive-in movies at least once a week, playing poker in the afternoon and making Chef Boyardee pizzas, and spending every free minute at our favorite hang-out, the D&B Restaurant on Main Street.

We looked a lot like the Burger Palace Boys from "Grease." We normally wore white tee shirts with blue jeans and several of my friends sported ducktails to finish off the look. We tucked our cigarettes into the sleeves of our tee shirts—just like Danny Zuko and Kenickie from the movie. I smoked Chesterfields, though there were lots of Camels and Lucky Strikes tucked into sleeves as well. No filtered cigarettes. That's what girls smoked.

The most memorable of my friends was Butchy Epifano, a "greaser" personified. (This is the same Butchy from the wiener roast incident.) His father owned the drive-in movie and a popular bar on Broadway. Butchy sported a mullet-like DA (duck ass, a longer version of ducktails), tight white tee that revealed his man-boobs, and a beer gut (a pity for a boy of 16!).

He had the foulest language of any of our gang, which we called "The Loafers." No matter what you said to Butchy, he had only one response: "Fuckin' A!"

"Hey Butch, you wanna get a burger?"

"Fuckin' A!"

"Hey fat ass, you wanna drag on Tile Plant Road?"

"Fuckin' A!"

While Butchy had a dirty mouth, he was the sweetest-smelling boy in New Lex. He literally must have bathed in Aqua Velva; his car was like stepping into an after-shave bottle.

Our gang of Loafers sat for hours on a ledge outside the entrance to the D&B. We passed the time by contributing to our large puddles of spittle. Each of us had our own little ponds in front of us. When we weren't smoking, spitting, and downing our Cokes, we were yelling at cars passing by, hopefully those containing our favorite girls. We ran into the street to stop them so we could impress the girls with our macho-ness and swear words. They seemed to buy our routine, which we repeated nightly.

I didn't hang out at the D&B much during "Freshmen Initiation" that summer because I knew what would happen. That was when every young man going into his freshman year had to avoid being caught by roving gangs of upperclassmen who found the opportunity to embarrass the hell out of him. The gang always found the perfect time to strike—when their potential victim was with a bunch of his friends.

Faster than you could say, "what the hell?" the freshman was pinned on the sidewalk as the upperclassmen removed his pants and ran through the streets to find a lamppost or flagpole on which to display them. The freshman had to know how to handle this attack. He could scream and swear but had to make sure not to fight back too vigorously. If he tried to hit, slap, or throw a punch, more than likely the underwear would come off right after the pants. It was humiliating, especially if you were with a pretty girl when the gang struck.

I willingly gave up my jeans on five occasions when I was an incoming freshman in the summer of 1958, but I never lost my tighty whities. I did sneak into my house twice without pants, even after running up and down Main Street and through all the upperclassmen's favorite "hanging" places looking for them. I lay low that summer, because I knew most of the guys, who were mainly from the public high school, would get a special pleasure from de-pantsing big shot Nick Missimi!

BUONE FESTE: MY THREE FAVORITE HOLIDAYS

The humdrum of everyday life for an Italian-American boy in small-town America was seasonal. I had my winter must-do lists—shoveling coal and snow—and my summer duties of watering the massive vegetable garden, washing the car, picking and canning tomatoes, and a long and endless list of my mom's household chores.

But Christmas, New Year's, and Easter celebrations gave me a great deal to look forward to. Each holiday was celebrated in true Italian fashion, featuring a menu of outstanding recipes and an equally impressive array of traditions.

With each holiday, I helped my family tailor-make the festivities to reflect the way my relatives had celebrated these special holiday/holydays back in Sicily and Apulia. Because of my bent for the theatrical, I always positioned myself to be an integral part of the holidays, helping my mom orchestrate the "banquet" elements and the necessary decorative aspects.

Little did I realize that I would put my years of holiday organizing experience—decorating the tree, playing Saint Nicholas with an audience of grade-school children, and prepping for our annual New Year's Eve super-spicy spaghetti party—to good use once I became a theatre professional. I spent my childhood on the stage of 714 North Main, surrounded by an unforgettable cast of characters and a setting that was right out of *It's a Wonderful Life*. Plus a coal mine and a few more farms.

The prequel to all this was Thanksgiving. An Italian-American Thanksgiving, to be sure, since in Italy there are many "giving thanks" celebrations for various saints and for the harvest, but no equivalent to Thanksgiving in the U.S.

Our holiday season always began with the War on Turkey at the end of November. I was in charge of keeping an eye on the turkey as it cooked. I insisted that my mom buy the largest turkey possible so it would look like the Norman Rockwell Thanksgiving dinner on the cover of *The Saturday Evening Post*. But year after year, my turkey choice proved to be too tight a fit for our antiquated oven. I spent hours on turkey vigil, listening to mom yelling "If you open that oven door one more time, I'll beat your ass!" and making sure the legs didn't stick to the inside of the oven. It was the battle of aluminum foil versus oven walls, but I always got pats on the back for a golden-colored bird, even with burnt drumsticks and a bit of missing skin.

Then December arrived and I was cast as Saint Nicholas—not in a play, but as the special visitor to all the classes of our grade school. I was a moderately tall eighth grader and had a kind voice and could talk easily with the younger children. Since Saint Nicholas was a bishop from Bari, Italy, the home of my grandparents and my mother, who better to impersonate the original gift-bearing Santa Claus than Nicky Missimi!

I donned a rather tattered red velvet robe, a fluffy white beard, and long, shoulder-length wig held in place with a bishop's mitre. I walked with an elaborate bishop's crozier; this helped give me a sense of authority, which I loved. I got to knock on every classroom door and present foil-wrapped candy bundles to the students. Accompanying me was the mischievous "Black Pit," one of the smaller students, with a tattered beggar's costume and a coal-blackened face. He brought along his pail with lumps of coal and when one of the nuns wanted to make a spectacle of the most-misbehaving student, she'd instruct my little sidekick to give the child a lump of coal. Cruel, I suppose, though the nun made sure the student (almost always a boy) eventually got his candy. But only after she cornered him for a good talking-to following the departure of Saint Nick.

Buon Natale! (Merry Christmas!)

There they were. Fifty pies—16 chocolate, 12 banana cream, 12 toasted coconut, and 10 pumpkin. This was my mom's over-the-top addition to the Christmas feast prepared at 714 North Main, and her bid for a little praise for cooking American desserts. The pies sat on the battered Amana freezer in the office, a small, attached, unheated room at the front of our house. They also covered the top of a normally cluttered wooden desk and a large, ancient Singer sewing machine. In the winter, the room temperature hovered around 45-50 degrees, a perfect storage room for Angie's holiday specialty.

The pies were made in reused, small Omar Bakery tins that barely yielded four slices, but they were a much-anticipated treat for the Missimi *famiglia* and the many immigrant neighbors who made a point of paying a visit, knowing that a slice of "heaven" would be offered by Angie. Mom's pies were created on Christmas Eve day with sister Regina, cousin Mary, and me serving as baking assistants. The first piece wasn't cut until everyone returned from midnight Mass, crowding around the kitchen's Formica table waiting for Angie to do the honors.

I was amazed that the pies made it to the table, considering who the head baker was. "Mom, why does this pudding taste so weird?" I said, pulling my finger from the bubbling kettle.

"What's wrong with it? I didn't do nothin' but mix the pudding and put some vanilla extract in it." She looked confused as I checked the bottle next to the kettle.

"Mom, this is Dr. Miles Nervine medicine. It's not vanilla."

"*Stronza!*" [turd], mom yelled. "I've got to have Dr. McDougal check my eyes!" And into the trash went the pudding for a dozen pies.

Another time, we stirred large vats of vanilla and chocolate pudding for close to an hour, until I discovered that mom had not read the box correctly and we were breaking our arms trying to thicken instant pudding.

Meringues were her major hurdle, though. Every Christmas, my mom desperately tried to keep the meringues from shrinking to something the size of a half dollar. "Not enough sugar?" "Did I beat the egg whites too long?" "Are the pies too close to the broiler?" No matter how many questions she asked, the meringue remained a sad little island marooned in the middle of a lake of pudding. No one complained. But while Angie was not always proud of her meringues, she knew she could hit a home run with Christmas dinner.

I woke every Christmas morning to the aroma of tomato sauce with meatballs, beef, and pork simmering in the kitchen below my bedroom. It was something I was used to. I had this same bit of olfactory heaven every Sunday, but on Christmas the "gravy" tasted even better, served atop mom's special pasta of seashell macaroni mixed with ricotta cheese brought from Columbus. As a kid, it was my favorite Italian dish.

Before I had to leave for the 10:30 Mass, I helped mom set the table for our feast. We didn't own anything fancy, though mom would splurge on Christmas paper napkins. It was one of the few days I put out our ruby red Venetian wine glasses. Oddly, while my Italian grandfather made several gallons of "dago red" every year, as a rule we didn't drink wine—only for special occasions or when company came to visit.

It was a typical holiday feast. Our *primo piatto* was pasta served with a mountain of meatballs, pork, and beef. Our *secundo* was baked chicken with rosemary-roasted potatoes and an enormous Italian salad with homemade bread. For *dolce*, in addition to Angie's pies, there were platters of Italian cookies and sometimes a *panetone* sent from Italy—that delicious sweet bread filled with candied fruits, chocolate chips, and nuts. There was handmade candy from Sicily, too—miniature marzipan fruits exquisitely fashioned but never eaten.

"Too pretty to eat!" mom told us. At Easter my Sicilian relatives often sent a marzipan Pascal lamb—even more beautiful, but also not for eating. What a pity that, after the holidays, it was my job to throw them all away, still uneaten.

We had dinner in the glow of the enormous Christmas tree that my dad and I had chopped down on the hills surrounding the Sunnyhill Coal Mine. Every year I begged for a tall, stately tree like I had seen in the magazines, but every year we cut four feet off the top to get it into the house.

Nicky and cousins Vickey and Mary

"It's too damn big, Dominic Eugene!" my mom yelled as we dragged it through the kitchen, knocking things off the table. Nevertheless, our Christmas "bush" was beautiful, almost as tall as it was wide, with its giant multi-colored lights, embossed, glitter-flocked balls, and tons of homemade ornaments I created, all shimmering under a veil of silver tinsel icicles.

"*Buon Natale*!" toasted my dad, carefully lifting his Venetian glass to our family and guests. The whole day was very Italian—too much food, too many pies, too many gaudy decorations, and not nearly enough holes in my Hopalong Cassidy belt. It all added up to my idea of a perfect Christmas.

Felice Anno Nuovo! (Happy New Year!)

Though Christmas was the highlight of the season, the six-week holiday period ended with a bang when the final moments of the year were celebrated with a volley of gunfire in the back yard of the Missimi house.

My family celebrated New Year's Eve exactly the same every year. I think it was a tradition begun by my grandfather. All our closest friends and neighbors who lived on Monument Square arrived at the house at 8 p.m.

The evening consisted of a loud, table-slapping card game played by the men in the kitchen with Italian decks of cards and an ever-growing cloud of tobacco smoke hovering over the players. "Goddam sunamabeech!" That was a phrase the players heard throughout the evening, as Grandpa Pete slammed another bad hand onto the table.

In the living room, a more refined gathering of Italian ladies downed glass after glass of their favorite licorice-flavored (anise) liqueur while perched as daintily as they could manage on Angie's exotic chairs, all decorated with starched lace doilies.

Two recurring events finished off the evening. First was a pepper-inspired tarantella danced by all the party-goers, induced by the intensely spiced spaghetti sauce served to everyone shortly before midnight. I was the "pepper boy," and my job was to drop dozens of hot peppers and their tongue-scorching seeds into the pasta "gravy." After only a few bites, the women began their dance, hopping up and down and waving their hands and shaking their aprons in front of their faces, skipping wildly to dispel the blazing spice. They laughed and screamed, hooted and slapped each other's backs, all while grabbing for cool bottles of beer or orange pop to put out the fire. The men never made a sound. They just sat there with tears running down their cheeks, dripping onto their plates of pasta. All this to the sound of Vic Damone singing "*O Sole Mio*" on our antiquated 78 rpm record player.

By the time my mom had screamed her final "*Jesù Cristo, troppo caldo*!" [too hot!] the family was heading to the back yard as the record changed to Guy Lombardo's "Auld Lang Syne." This was the finale of the old year—one final boom.

Only a few of my uncles owned guns. They used them mainly for hunting rabbits around Thanksgiving time. Regina's husband Ralphie had wanted a new gun, so Regina saved to buy him one for Christmas and now he had a chance to try it out.

After a night of unending laughter from the super-spicy pasta, Ralphie found a way to cap the evening's festivities. He blew off two of his fingers.

I don't remember if they rushed him to the hospital, if someone had the sense to pick up his fingers and take them with him, but whatever happened, he did not come out of the ordeal with all his digits. In fact, Ralphie, who was always "Mr. Jokester," made sure he shook your hand every time he met you. He liked to wiggle the missing stumps, so you felt the movement of what was missing. He grinned and said, "I guess you gave me five and I gave you three." It was never funny, but Ralphie was such a unique little guy—a perfect twin to the 1950s television actor Wally Cox ("Mr. Peepers")—that you had to smile back at him and say, "You're funny, Ralphie."

I only recently discovered that Ralph and Regina's children were told a different story—that he had lost his fingers in a factory accident when a machine press smashed them. But I was there when Ralphie shot off his gun to ring in the New Year. He certainly made 1958 go out with a bang, even though I recall that he left the festivities with a whimper.

Buona Pasqua! (Happy Easter!)

My dad was one of the world's least likely Easter Bunnies. He didn't dress up in a bunny costume with long pink ears and carry a stuffed carrot in his white furry mitten-paw. He didn't wear a costume at all, but my dad imbued the spirit of that lovable holiday icon with total commitment. He looked upon his job of hiding Easter eggs as one of the highlights of his dull coal miner's life.

On all but one day of the year, my dad dressed in coal-stained work pants, a faded, over-washed flannel shirt, work boots, and a dingy baseball cap. He could get through the day without a smile, never spoke more words than were absolutely necessary, and often replaced "yes" and "no" with a grunt or a shake of his head. He wasn't big on interpersonal communication. I think he was mostly tired since his day on his truck started at 4:30 a.m. when he left for Sunnyhill Coal Mine to load up for his first delivery of the day.

But on Easter morning, he slept until 5 a.m., dressed in a pair of gabardine pants, a pressed cotton shirt, and his church shoes, and topped it all off with his fedora. He skipped breakfast to get out in the yard as the sun was rising. On Holy Saturday my mom dyed several dozen eggs, most destined for the hunt but some twisted into the sweet bread called *pane di pasqua*—also a tradition for most Italian families at Eastertime.

Dad gathered up his basket of colored eggs and used a wax pen to write numbers on some of them. There were about 10 with "1" written on them, 5 with "5," and only 1 with "10." This is the number of dollars the children would receive from their Grandpa Guy once they "cashed in" their eggs at the end of the hunt. Many eggs had no numbers on them. They were there just for the fun of finding them and were returned to Grandma Angie's enormous bowl of pastel eggs. Just like the meringues my mom could never figure out how to keep from shrinking, she could never figure out how to get the eggs to take the dye and turn into the ruby reds, cerulean blues, and lemon yellows she saw pictured on the egg-dye package.

"Maybe I should use more vinegar," she lamented. "Next year you color 'em, Nicky. I can't do 'em worth a damn!"

Dad had many favorite hiding places that we older kids knew very well. He liked to plant eggs in the downspouts and under the Maytag washing machine against the kitchen wall under the grape arbor. There were eggs behind the statue of Saint Anthony in our outdoor shrine, eggs in Fuzzy's doghouse, eggs hidden behind Grandpa's fig—but please don't touch that precious tree!

Easter egg hunters

My brother's and sister's kids arrived around 11:30 a.m., following the 10:30 Mass. The girls held a "fashion parade" to show off their beautiful new Easter dresses and lacy bonnets with pink and white ribbons. Every boy squirmed in his sport coat and necktie, waiting breathlessly to be given permission to remove them for the egg hunt. Mom and the wives stayed in the kitchen to put final touches on the Easter feast and Guy, his children, and

12 grandchildren were poised and ready to begin the hunt, waiting for Grandpa Guy to give them the word.

"Okay everybody, listen to me." My dad was not used to speaking to a group, even a group of children under the age of 10. "I hid the eggs all over the yard. If you find one with a number on it, bring it to me and I'll give you the money that's written on the egg. Nicky, you get the Easter hunt started."

I think my dad was too embarrassed to say, "On your mark, get set, go!" and just as I was ready to say it, the front door slammed open and mom came barreling out into the yard.

"Now listen to me!" she shouted. "Your mom and dad spent a lot of money on your nice Easter clothes, so make sure you don't roll around in the grass and get stains on your knees."

"Okay, Grandma!" The kids were eager to get started. But mom wasn't done yet.

"And don't tear anything, you hear me? Dinner will be ready in a half hour! And don't bug your grandpa. He's been up since five hiding these damn eggs! You hear me?"

"Okay, Grandma," the children yelled.

Before she could get another word in, I yelled out "On your mark, get set, go!" And the search was on.

I watched my dad during the egg hunt. To my knowledge, he had never played any kind of sports. But this was the moment he could play referee. He ignored the older kids who knew their way around the yard and the hunt, but he coached the four- and five-year olds—Patti, Lisa, Steve, and Mary—constantly saying

"You're getting warmer, warmer. No, no, no, you're getting cold, getting colder…." And he smiled, more smiles than you'd see on his face in a whole year. This was his famous Easter Sunday smile.

The hunt never lasted more than 30 minutes. The children brought their eggs to Grandpa Guy and cashed them in for their rewards. "Put all the eggs with no numbers in the bowl. Grandma's looking forward to making her potato salad with those eggs."

The colored eggs sat on our kitchen counter for weeks, except for the dozen my mother chopped into her favorite Italian potato salad, speckled with bits of fresh basil. After two weeks, they were tossed out with the garbage (just like the Christmas and Easter marzipans). None of us liked plain hard-boiled eggs. So we had to wait another year for the pale-colored orbs to become the most important part of our Easter celebration. And it would be another year before we would have the pleasure of enjoying the once-a-year grin and twinkly eyes of the master of the hunt, my dad.

PART TWO

Crescere

(Grown Up)

A LIFE IN THE THEATRE

Elementary School

In the sixth grade I first considered joining the world of make-believe. Sitting in the auditorium at Saint Aloysius Academy with my classmates from Saint Rose of Lima Elementary School, I watched *The Song of Bernadette.* The play was pretty boring for the first half hour. And then something magical happened. The young Bernadette knelt before a large stone grotto. It was not painted expertly but it certainly created the illusion of a primitive cave formed with gray and black rocks. A celestial melody began and ever so gradually the stage lights faded as a transformation took place. The stones melted away and the vision of the Madonna appeared. She was clothed in a brilliant blue mantle, her hair covered with a white veil and golden roses at her feet. Is this really happening? I thought. Is she really appearing before us? Is this a miracle?

At the end of the performance my brother Tony, one of the cast members, took me backstage to show me the scrim, a painted cloth used to create the illusion of the appearance of Mary. It had totally fooled me. I'd been certain that I had watched a miracle. The image of that transformation haunted me for days, and ultimately inspired me to become part of a world that created "miracles" on stage.

My next theatrical experience involved a trip to Columbus to see a Kenley Players summer stock performance of *Where's Charley?*—the musical version of *Charley's Aunt.* Everything about the Kenley Players impressed me. I never would have guessed that three years later I'd come back to that theatre as a professional apprentice. The theatre seated 3,000 people, which I found astounding. The stage was enormous, filled with wonderful scenic elements—turntables in the floor, painted drops, moving wagons, and imaginative props. I had never seen professional scenery before and it delighted me. I wanted to be up there. I wanted to be part of the world that brought such pleasure to the audience.

That same year I decided to write a musical, *Holly and Ivy*, based on a story I read in Regina's copy of *Good Housekeeping* magazine. It took place in a magical toy shop where all the dolls come to life. When I approached Sister Rosalie, my eighth-grade teacher, to tell her about my project, she shocked me by saying she would present the musical to the Parent Teacher Association as a special Christmas entertainment.

I couldn't play the piano. I had once convinced my mom to allow me to accept an offer of a massive upright, even though it practically ruptured my friends and me as we hoisted it up a flight of stairs to get it onto Regina's front porch. Mom wouldn't let me put it in our house, so in the winter, I'd be at Regina's "composing" in the snow. I plunked out melodies, memorized them, and taught them to my classmates for my big composer/playwright debut.

I also decided to choreograph the show, with what meager knowledge I had about dancing, thinking I could duplicate some of the ideas I had seen in *Where's Charley?*

Getting ready for an afternoon rehearsal, I felt a strange ache behind my ears. It was bothersome but I decided to ignore it. I spent most of my staging rehearsal teaching the "toys" to jump off the shelves in the toy shop and reviewed over and over the simple march steps I had devised for the scene. Exhausted from the rehearsal, I decided to take a hot bath before bed. As I was getting out of the tub, I realized the pain that had been throbbing behind my ears had disappeared. I also realized the pain now had descended into my nether region and was proving more painful than when it lived behind my ears. It was the mumps, and they had dropped into my testicles. Only after a trip to the hospital and several needle punctures to drain the fluid was I relieved of my testicular "elephantiasis."

I returned to normal just in time for my triumphant theatrical debut. What a dreadful little production it must have been! I still remember a few of the songs—"Wishing is a Thing of Magic" and the title song "Holly and Ivy." They were nice enough. But I can't imagine how we did an original musical with no musical accompaniment, not even a piano. Then again, perhaps we were 60 years ahead of the trend—an *a capella* musical in 1958!

High School

My high school years were filled with more theatrical successes. I appeared regularly in a variety of high school-ish plays but was thrilled to be featured in the old chestnut, *The Barretts of Wimpole Street*, in which I played the stern Papa Barrett, the joyless father of Elizabeth Barrett Browning and her many siblings. I topped off my high school career as Saint Peter in *The Big Fisherman*, based on the popular film. Throughout my four years I also was called upon to write countless skits and lyrics for a variety of occasions. With these special programs I began to develop my interest in direction, since I also was in charge of staging my original material.

Perhaps my oddest theatrical creation was a benefit performance of *Around the World in Eighty Days*. It was a water ballet! We swam to the soundtrack of the 1956 Oscar-winning film with music by Victor Young. As president of the Catholic Youth Organization I was determined to find a way to raise money for Catholic missions in Africa and Asia.

Our water ballet took place in the municipal pool and featured a cast of high school swimmers. After all, I was the "basket boy" at the pool, checking everyone's clothes, and I knew all the lifeguards and other workers. I recruited the best divers and high school athletes—knowing that my jock friends would provide an excellent band of clowns to entertain from the high diving board.

After watching several Esther Williams movies, I enlisted the public-school girls to help create synchronized swimming routines. Across Mechanic Street from my house was Cheney's tire shop. All the tires were shipped and wrapped in brightly colored plastic—red, blue, and yellow. This wonderfully crisp plastic could be sewn, and I recruited a few girls in my class to create costumes the swimmers could wear during their routines. The material never wrinkled and retained its crispness in the water—perfect plastic tutus!

The main event was the girls' synchronized swimming, featuring a series of multi-colored scenes and movements reflecting the dancing styles of many countries in Europe, plus China, India, Thailand, and others. The comic relief was provided by the boys. We were dressed in 1920s bathing beauty costumes from the French Riviera, borrowed from St. Al's. I remember my beauty-contest Nicaraguan girlfriend yelling through the cyclone fence—"Oh, Neeeky! You so cute in you costoom!" We looked ridiculous, and the costumes gave us the courage to perform our stunts with total abandon as we hurled ourselves off the high board. I don't remember how much money we raised for the missions, but the event was a big success for the young Italian showman.

By the time senior year came around, I had to finalize my plans for college. I couldn't possibly tell my parents I wanted them to pay the tuition for a theatre major! Many of my high school projects involved journalism. I was editor of the school newspaper and the literary magazine, *Crescendo*. I had attended a number of journalism workshops and had received a scholarship from the University of Detroit, a Jesuit institution, in exchange for work on their publications. It was much easier to tell my family I was going to major in journalism, with my hope of becoming a theatre critic. At least it sounded like a field in which I might actually find a job that would provide an income.

College

My freshman year at the University of Detroit in 1962 convinced me more than ever that I wanted a life in the theatre.

Coincidentally, Detroit was experiencing a "golden age" of performing arts and I was a close-up witness to this renaissance. As a rookie theatre critic for the *Varsity News*, the school's daily newspaper, I saw the world premieres of *Hello Dolly!, Fiddler on the Roof*, and dozens of other shows that became major Broadway successes. In addition, I was introduced to the world of dance and found myself sitting in the best seats for the Kirov Ballet, the Bolshoi Ballet, and American Ballet Theatre. Added to that, imagine the thrill of a week of full-scale Metropolitan Opera performances with a roster of international stars.

After attending a much more intimate performance at the U of D theatre, however, I was hooked. How could a small-town coal miner's son be overwhelmed by a production of Sophocles' *Electra* performed in a tiny theatre on the top floor of the school library? The actors were wonderful, and I wanted desperately to be one of them.

In my sophomore year I declared my theatre major and enrolled in my first acting classes. I never told my parents. They were uneducated and could barely write their names and do basic addition, let alone read a transcript of my classes and grades. I wasn't sure they would grasp the difference between Introduction to Print Journalism and Basic Acting Skills.

But one day my mom shared with me a secret that helped cement my decision to pursue a career in theatre.

When I came home for Christmas during my freshman year, mom asked me to sit down at the kitchen table just as I was heading out the door with my luggage. I was eager to hit the road to Columbus to catch the Amtrak back to Detroit.

"Nicky honey, sit down. I wanna tell you something."

I noticed she had an apologetic expression on her face. "What's up, Mom?"

She spoke carefully, weighing her words, wishing not to let her message spill out with too much intensity—something she normally did, even if she was telling me what she was cooking for supper.

"I never told you this before, honey. When I was a little girl, carnivals and sometimes a little circus would come to our town of Noicàttaro. Grandpa and Grandma had no money for me to go to the shows, but the actors would often preview their performance in the piazza under the *campanile* [bell tower]."

"Really? You remember that?"

"Oh yes, *lo ricordo* [I remember] and I loved it! I wanted to be one of those pretty dancers in their beautiful costumes, twirling on the cobblestones and singing like birds! I'd chase after them when they were done doing their show. I just wanted to touch their costumes and have them smile at me."

"That sounds wonderful, Mom! I guess you had stars in your eyes like your son!"

"Oh, it was wonderful. So you see, honey, you got your crazy idea about being an actor from your mom. That's what I dreamed of—joining the circus." She chuckled and gave me one of her looks that told me we were having a moment. "*Sono pazzo* [I'm crazy!], just like you, you little shithead!" Another one of her favorite expressions of endearment.

"Thanks for telling me, Mom. I've always thought you and Regina belonged on stage!"

The highlight of my sophomore year was an apprenticeship with the Kenley Players in Columbus. As apprentices we did whatever was asked of us, from working backstage to sending complimentary tickets to addresses in the Columbus phone book. If a small role needed to be filled, an apprentice often was assigned to perform.

In the summer of 1964, I made my professional acting debut in two very small roles. I was a Guard—no lines—in *A Shot in the Dark* with Eva Gabor (star of TV's *Green Acres*), and the Plumber in *Never Too Late* with Arthur Godfrey (a popular radio and television entertainer) and Maureen O'Sullivan (most famous as Jane in several *Tarzan* movies).

Ms. Gabor seemed to have it in for me, telling the producer I was spying on her in her dressing room (her imagination, most definitely). I inadvertently got my revenge. On opening night, when she stepped forward to announce the winning numbers of a ticket that would give the recipient a beautiful necklace from Mama Gabor's jewelry line, I whispered in her ear the winning number. She stepped forward dramatically to announce the winner. Unfortunately, I was standing on the hem of her costume and her giant step forward ripped out the entire back of her gown. She refused to look at me for the remainder of the run, which was just fine with me.

On the other hand, Arthur Godfrey was a gem, a lovely gentleman and a good friend to the crew. With my apprentice buddies we often swam with him in the elegant pool at his hotel. He also hosted a magnificent Hawaiian luau at the Kahiki Supper Club for the cast and crew, and even brought his famous ukulele to serenade the company. The summer was a whirlwind of hanging around the stars of our shows—singer Robert Goulet and his stage actress/singer/wife Carol Lawrence, crooner Jack Jones, sex-pot Jayne Mansfield, and many others.

Best of all, at the end of the season, the producer asked me to assist the director of the final production, *Lady in the Dark*. It was the directing debut of famed dancer and choreographer Jacques D'Amboise, one of America's premiere male dancers from the New York City Ballet. I spent the entire week taking notes for Mr. D'Amboise and every moment with this brilliant artist deepened my resolve to have theatre and dance as a part of my life.

Nick as Truffaldino

My acting career at the University of Detroit included a number of wonderful roles. Most notable was that of Mr. Zuss (God) in *J.B.*, Archibald MacLeish's poetic retelling of the story of Job and his wife Sarah. In my senior year, I starred in the classic *commedia dell'arte* play, *The Servant of Two Masters* by Italian playwright Carlo Goldoni, playing the mischievous servant, Truffaldino. It was a role I was built to play and I reveled in this famous clown's stylish, dancerly comedy.

DOMINIC MISSIMI

Actor/Director/Choreographer

Size: 46R
Height: 5'11"
Weight: 230
Hair: Dk. Brown
Eyes: Dk. Brown
Waist: 40
Inseam: 31
Shirt: 17-33
Shoe: 10

I had hundreds of these acting composites printed in 1980, one week before I got my full-time teaching job at Northwestern. So much for my acting career....

In 1967, the chairman of the University of Detroit Theatre Department asked me to join the faculty. I was flabbergasted. I was going to be a college teacher and I'd only received my bachelor's degree a year before! Of course, there was a hitch. The Theatre Department had very little money, so I agreed to teach for $5,000 a year. But money was not important. Having the opportunity to continue to sharpen my teaching and directing skills was the main benefit, and the possibility of working toward my master's degree at Wayne State University provided the extra incentive to say "Yes, yes, yes! I want the job!"

And thus my theatre and directing career began in earnest. I spent 10 years at U of D, eventually chairing the department and creating a dance major and a dance company called DANCE DETROIT. I followed that with three years in New York City, working on my doctorate at New York University and teaching and directing at the C.W. Post campus of Long Island University, while traveling regularly to direct operas for many of America's regional companies. I had the good fortune to work with a number of star performers, including Ed Asner (*The Mary Tyler Moore Show*), comics Imogene Coca and Dick Shawn, Barbara Eden (*I Dream of Jeannie*), and Oscar-winner Rita Moreno (Anita in *West Side Story*).

Rita Moreno in Marriott's Scapino

In 1980, following a move to Chicago, I began my association with Northwestern University and a professional career of directing musicals and operas throughout the U.S. I established a music theatre program and founded a "new works" program called the American Music Theatre Project. I became a regular director at one of Chicago's premier playhouses, the Marriott Theatre at Lincolnshire, where I won several prestigious Joseph Jefferson Awards for my productions and direction.

For many years, I served as President and Artistic Director of the Sarah Siddons Society, a Chicago-based theatrical organization begun in the early 1950s by a group of avid first-night Chicago theatregoers. The society annually presents its prestigious acting award to an outstanding American actor. For the past 30 years, I have staged musical programs and arranged elaborate awards ceremonies to honor Barbara Cook, Audra McDonald, Bernadette

Peters, Patti LuPone, Sutton Foster, Julie Andrews, and many other film, television, and Broadway stars.

Nick, Audra McDonald, and Stephen Sondheim at Chicago Shakespeare benefit

My Northwestern students were some of America's smartest and most talented. I was particularly happy to have directed a number of future Hollywood stars while they were undergrads, though their roles were unmemorable, to say the least. I cast David Schwimmer (*Friends*) as the rear end of a donkey in a children's musical I wrote, and Stephen Colbert (*Late Night with Stephen Colbert*) was the third Eskimo from the left in my production of *The Ice Wolf.* Greg Berlanti (now one of Hollywood's most successful producers, with dozens of major TV series to his credit) played a secondary role, Barnaby, in my production of Thornton Wilder's *The Matchmaker.*

I count many of my former students, both from the University of Detroit and Northwestern, as some of my dearest friends.

Fun with NU students at Cubs game

My retirement from Northwestern was celebrated with a splendid evening of entertainment called "Starry, Starry Night." The cast of 250 consisted of Broadway performers, many of Chicago's major music theatre artists, and members of the university's music theatre and opera programs. It was thrilling to see several of my famous former students on stage, including Tony winner Heather Headley, multiple-Tony nominee Brian Darcy James, plus former Miss America Kate Shindle.

For the finale, the enormous cast sang one of my all-time favorites— "Make Our Garden Grow" from Leonard Bernstein's *Candide.* I sat next to my wife and daughters, my brother Tony and cousin Mary right behind me, and 1,000 former students and theatre friends filling Cahn Auditorium. Tears ran down my cheeks. My career at Northwestern had been filled with some of my most rewarding moments in the theatre. And there were many of them—right up on stage in front of me—singing at me, "This is your life, Dominic Missimi!"

NANCY

I've known Nancy for nearly 60 years. In 2019 we celebrated our 50th wedding anniversary, but I met her six years before our marriage.

I was beginning my sophomore year at the University of Detroit and, having recently declared my theatre major, was making my first trip to the Theatre Department on the third floor of the library. This would be my new home on campus, no longer shackled to my desk in the Journalism Department writing for the daily newspaper and working on the yearbook.

The theatre wasn't impressive. There were 124 folding chairs and a platform stage surrounded by black velour curtains. The surrounding walls were beige curtains that hid all the bookcases that remained from the theatre's former life as a library reference room. Most enjoyable for me was the long, cluttered room adjoining the theatre. This was the "green room," the traditional name for the actors' meeting place, though there wasn't a lick of green anywhere, only the landscape of treetops visible through the wall of windows. Connected to the green room was the tiny costume shop with clothes racks and sewing machines crammed together. That was where I first met Nancy.

She was sitting at a sewing machine and seemed to be an experienced seamstress, feeding the fabric expertly through the machine. I introduced myself. She looked up, smiled, and said her name was Nancy Dudka. That's a funny name, I thought. Maybe she's Polish, like so many of the students I've met at U of D. She had wonderfully blonde hair and my first impression was that she could have been the sister of Mary Travers, a member of one of my favorite groups, Peter, Paul and Mary. She had very pretty eyes and a big smile, just like the song I knew by Jimmy Van Heusen, "Nancy (with the Laughing Face)." Later I learned that the song was written the year I was born, 1944. Kismet! But our meeting was brief and Nancy quickly went back to her work. I left the green room thinking about her.

She definitely was pretty, very kind, and somewhat reserved. I looked forward to seeing her again. I'd run into her every time I came for acting classes. There she was, sewing with great skill and concentration at her trusty little Singer sewing machine. One day, I arrived at the same time she did. When I saw her walk from the coatrack to the sewing machine, I noticed she had a limp. I wouldn't learn until later, once we began dating, that she had contracted polio when she was young and spent many months in the hospital. Her impediment didn't seem to bother her. I soon learned that she could do pretty much anything anyone else could do.

Everyone was abuzz with talk about the upcoming Halloween Costume Ball, an annual event for The Players, an organization of students and alumni of the Theatre Department. My first thought was: who better to take to the Costume Ball than a professional seamstress? So I asked Nancy to be my date for the big shindig.

I'd say we were the belle and beau of the ball. We went as Napoleon and Josephine. Nancy found me an excellent period costume in the storage room and fashioned a beautiful, sky-blue Empire gown for her Josephine costume. She was beautiful, and with her blonde hair piled high on her head she certainly looked the part of an Empress.

Our courtship spanned six years. During that time, I graduated from U of D, taught at a ritzy all-girl high school, joined the theatre faculty at U of D, and got my Master's in Theatre from Wayne State University. Nancy also graduated from U of D—*summa cum laude*, no less—got her Master's in English, and was promoted to head costumer for the Theatre Department.

We spent our free time going to movies and eating at most of the Polish and Italian restaurants in Detroit. An added bonus was the time I spent at Nancy's house with her mom, Helen. I looked forward to our dates, but I also looked forward to the post-date special treat waiting for me in her mom's kitchen. Nancy's mom seemed to take great pleasure in preparing minute steaks with onions and green peppers for my late-night snack. Even after I had dinner with Nancy, this 10 p.m. mini-meal was a perfect end to the day.

We were married on April 26, 1969. It was my mom's dream to have her little Nicky married, with the prospect of a son to come who would carry on the family name. My only Missimi brother was a Catholic priest so I was her only hope. The wedding was held at Nancy's Detroit parish, Saint Francis De Sales, and my entire family came from Ohio to celebrate—my parents, my brother Louis and his six kids, brother Pete with his son and daughter, and sister Regina with her four. The rest of the Italian contingent came in from Bellevue and Cleveland and all Nancy's relatives came from Flint and the Detroit suburbs. With our many friends from the university, we had a sizable crowd.

Since both of our parents' finances were modest, Nancy and I did everything we could to make it a reasonable affair. Our reception venue was a far cry from the many lovely banquet halls Nancy and I had been to at our friends' weddings. We chose the VFW Hall. It certainly was nothing fancy, but with mountains of Italian and Polish sausages, huge pans of pasta and meatballs, and my favorite—Nancy's Uncle Louie's famous stuffed cabbage—it was an Italian-Polish feast. A thrown-together rock band was assembled from our friends in the Theatre Department and while we danced into the wee hours, some of the Ohio guests spent the last half of the evening checking out the strip bars on Telegraph Road.

Our wedding with my siblings and their spouses

Nancy and I spent the next 10 years advancing our careers. She took over as costume designer for the Theatre Department and I began to work for professional theatres and opera companies in addition to my teaching and directing duties at U of D. Within a few years we purchased our first home, a small and wonderful cross-timbered Tudor in a park-like setting.

We spent 1971-72 in Europe—one of the best years of our lives. I received a Kellogg Fellowship from the cereal folks, which gave me my annual salary with no strings attached. In fact, the fellowship forbade me from pursuing graduate studies. It was to be a year of re-invigoration in teaching and the exploration of new coursework. We bought a new VW "Bug" that we picked up in Frankfurt before settling in our charming mews apartment in the Paddington neighborhood of London—one room, no television, no radio, coin-operated hot water system—snugly situated in a former stable.

It was like a really long honeymoon for Nancy and me. We went to the theatre six times a week and took classes and workshops when we weren't tooling around in our Bug or downing pints of "bitter" in our "local." One of our favorite activities was searching out good lunch bargains. Regularly, we could find three courses—soup, main course, and a delicious dessert of jelly roll with warm custard—for 30 pence (75 cents). Such a deal!

Nancy even started to talk with a British accent. It was a glorious year, and Nancy and I looked the best we ever had.

I was most amazed by Nancy's astounding strength and endurance. We couldn't afford to sit on the main floor when we went to the theatre. We'd usually pay 50 pence (about $1.25) to sit up in "the gods" with our heads almost touching the ceiling. It was our decision to go to every show possible rather than spending a bundle on a single performance. That meant walking up five to six flights of stairs to get to our cheap seats. While we went slowly and rested at the landings, Nancy never complained. She was a champ and could do everything I did, including descending all the steps to get to the "Tube," London's subway, in the stations where there was no escalator.

When we traveled abroad in our spiffy, bright-blue Bug, we stayed in the shabbiest accommodations—often on the third or fourth floor. It was all we could afford because we wanted to spend our money seeing the sights. We celebrated Mass with the Pope in Saint Peter's, cried as we floated down the Grand Canal in Venice, were dazzled by Chagall's brilliant ceiling at the Paris Opera, held our breaths as we drove through the tunnels of Mont Blanc in the dead of winter, and giggled when we were welcomed with open arms by my Sicilian family. It truly was a year to remember, and I was so proud to have my beautiful wife beside me. Besides, she was a great driver! It was Nancy who drove over the Alps in winter, taking us from London to Sicily. She hated my driving.

A few years after we returned to Detroit, we set our sights on New York City, the center of our theatrical world. Astonishingly, we found a lovely brownstone apartment on the Upper West Side—two bedrooms, parquet floors, a small eat-in kitchen, and a view of a beautiful back garden—just a few blocks from Lincoln Center. We were the envy of everyone who visited us. While I attended doctoral classes at New York University and free-lanced as a director, Nancy landed a spectacular job as head of the Costume Collection for the Theatre Development Fund. The job had some fantastic fringe benefits, namely that Nancy was invited to most opening nights on Broadway. The chance to see three years of great Broadway theatre, in primo seats, was close to miraculous.

Following our stint in New York and a very short residency at a professional theatre in northern Indiana, Nancy and I agreed it was time to give up our gypsy life, stay in once place, and focus on having children. After several years of trying to get pregnant, we realized we needed to take a different path to parenthood, so we pursued adoption. I knew Nancy was concerned that she would have a hard time keeping up with a toddler, but I assured her that I would be her legs. By the time we got our life organized so we could make room for children, I was 46 and Nancy was 45. Even at this "advanced age" we began the adoption procedures that would help us bring home two magnificent babies—our daughters Mary Elizabeth and Angela.

Emmy's first Halloween—Scarlett O'Hara

There was no end to people's comments when they met our two girls, mostly along the lines of "Oh, you have such beautiful grandchildren!"

"No," we'd say, "they're our kids. We just waited a little longer for our reward!"

I got my reward more than 50 years ago when I married Nancy. She shames me with her goodness and humility. She is kindness personified. She is devoted to our daughters and has been a caring and loving wife and friend. She is the person I respect more than any other. She has pain in her life—every day, in fact—but she never complains.

I have a long, long list of faults. She has only one: she talks loudly in her sleep. That's it. I'm a very lucky man and have been blessed to have shared my life with this exceptional woman. I love you, Nancy.

DOMENICO IN SICILY

As a grand finale to our year abroad, Nancy and I traveled in the summer of 1972 to the sunny island of Sicily in our VW Bug. Our final destination was the land of the Missimi *famiglia.*

With green faces, we ferried and bounced our way across an angry English Channel to Calais. With Nancy at the wheel, we traversed the Alps again—no less terrifying than in winter—and cautiously tunneled through Mont Blanc, teeth grinding and faces now bloodless and white.

This trip was our second to Italy. We'd had fantastic experiences seeing all the sites in *la bell' Italia* earlier in our sabbatical year. This trip to Sicily was strictly family. And what a comedy sketch!

My 15-year old sister-in-law Lisanne joined Nancy and me in Rome, in itself a remarkable experience for three people who barely spoke a word of Italian. Lisanne spent the majority of the time in Rome, and, in fact, of the entire 10-day trip, snuggled in the back seat of the Bug, barely conscious.

"Look, Lisanne, it's the Spanish Steps!" Nancy said to the lump in the back seat.

"Oh, yeah. That's cool." And the blanket went back over her head.

"Look, Lisanne, It's the Colosseum!" No response. "Wake up, Lisanne. We're at the Vatican!"

"You go. I'm tired!" she moaned, embracing her pillow and blanket.

"Leave her alone," I said. "She can see it when she's 30."

We made it out of Rome alive and eventually found our way onto the autostrada that would take us to Sicily. We drove south through several regions, the sun warming us up and restoring color to our cheeks. When we finally disembarked from the ferry at Messina, we had arrived on that magical island. In a few minutes and a few miles, we would be greeted by the warm embraces of the Missimi clan in their little village of Sant'Agata di Militello.

As we approached the village, Lisanne seemed much more alert. I think it was the prospect of meeting my four male teenage cousins. Perhaps this is where her European adventure would begin. Enough with these dumb old monuments and scary towns!

When we found Sant'Agata, we were somewhat shocked that my uncle's house was directly on the street. I mean right on the street—maybe four feet from the cars passing dangerously close to the door. I double parked and put on my emergency lights and planned to go to the door to announce our arrival. No sooner had I climbed out than the street was alive with aunts, uncles, cousins, and neighbors all swarming around our car. My cousin Antonio (the fifth Tony Missimi in the family) directed traffic around our street-side reunion as we all took turns receiving the standard two-cheek-three-kiss greeting followed by rib-shattering hugs from every member of my family. It was just as I imagined it would be.

"*Domenico! Che bello!*" [How handsome!] shouted my Aunt Anna. My eyes bugged out as I stared at my aunt's clothing. She was a recent widow and every piece of clothing was black, including small bits of material that covered her earrings. She was one of those scary women you saw in travel books about Calabria and Sicily, spying through the curtains at every foreign face that had the audacity to invade their village.

With the exception of my Aunt Anna, all the women looked like my *Nonna* (Grandma) Maria who had come to America 40 years earlier. That meant frumpy house dresses, faded floral wrap-around aprons, peasant babushkas, and backless house slippers. In contrast, the men wore nicely pressed shirts, pleated woolen trousers, and well-made leather shoes. That was how the men dressed for an afternoon of card-playing and wine-drinking and trips to *il bar* to meet up with their *compares*. While the women slaved in their ancient houses, the men seemed to do nothing. To my knowledge, the men had no real jobs. It made me a little nervous. It didn't take long for these scenes of Sicilian life to begin to look a great deal like scenes from *The Godfather*. I wasn't going to ask any questions.

Our visit was packed with precious memories: watching my female cousins baking in the outdoor ovens attached to their cream-colored stucco houses; sleeping in a bedroom with a sheepskin coverlet and woven twigs that formed the ceiling; the white ceramic pot that was the toilet in the kitchen. When I snuck into the kitchen at 2 a.m. to let nature take its course, I found the pot surrounded by a family of mice. I hopped back into our shepherd's bed, deciding Nancy and I would need to find a gas station with a bathroom in the morning.

One of the most memorable and touching aspects of life in Italy is the nightly stroll—the *passeggiata*. We did our promenade along the waterfront with everyone arm in arm and neighbors jostling to meet the *Americani* newly arrived in their village. The harbor waters were alive with silver-skinned anchovies, reflecting the setting sun.

Lisanne was all smiles, having won the attention of my most handsome cousin. He returned her smiles, grinning madly and inching closer and closer to the pretty blonde, surrounded by a wall of his sisters. And then his mother, Aunt Rosalina, slammed her purse into the side of his head and gave Lisanne the *mal'occhio*—the evil eye. Lisanne quickly learned that young ladies should look only straight ahead, paying no attention to the horny young men of my family, whether it was Antonio or Antonio or Antonio.

Aunt Rosalina and Aunt Maria were stunned the day after our arrival when they realized I was not wearing a wedding band, especially since Nancy and I had been married just a few years before. I tried to explain that I had lost my ring when I dove into the Adriatic in the resort town of Rimini. The two women screamed to their husbands, Uncle Joe and Uncle Charlie, "*Che disgrazia*!" [What a disgrace!]

Immediately, Nancy and I were escorted into town to visit the local goldsmith. No married nephew of theirs was going to advertise to the world that he was a single man. I tried on a simple gold band and it fit perfectly. "*Bene*," I said to my uncles, "*è perfetto*," I added sheepishly, trying out a few words of Italian. "*Quanto costa*?" Uncle Joe piped in, with a threatening look at the shopkeeper, who placed the ring on a scale. How amazing that there was no price tag on the ring; the gold needed to be weighed. I don't remember what the goldsmith said, but at the mention of the price, all hell broke loose in the tiny shop.

My aunts screamed "*Sei pozzo*!" [You're crazy!] and the uncles slammed their fists on the counter as Uncle Joe threw the ring at the goldsmith. "*Vaffuncuola*!" the men yelled, accompanied by the appropriate arm gesture that clearly matched the sentiment "Up yours!" This band of gypsies stormed out of the shop, spilling onto the street and hurling their insults back through the door with the ringing bell.

But they knew what they were doing. In about 20 seconds, the goldsmith was standing at the door, beckoning to us to reenter his shop for further negotiations. After a few more false exits and several more curses, Aunt Rosalina slipped the ring onto the finger of her red-faced nephew as Aunt Maria slipped a second ring onto Nancy's finger. They wanted us to have a matching pair.

I stared at Nancy. She was totally flabbergasted, and her expression was a mixture of fear, amazement, and gratitude. I'm sure we were thinking the same thing—is this band of crazed gypsies really my family? Yes, they are. But for someone who had devoted his life to the theatre, I could not imagine a more convincing group of actors who knew exactly how to get what they wanted! I'm happy to say that since that day I have never taken the ring off my finger.

Sicily was unforgettable and the experience of a lifetime. How could this mysterious island be so rough and so Baroque at the same time? From the outside, my family were peasants—simple houses, simple food, simple clothing. But on the inside, there often were surprises—a Madonna in an ornate 18th century frame, an exquisitely carved wall of cabinetry, richly colored pottery at the table.

2016 reunion with Sicilian cousins

My family's romantic love and affection was as rich and curlicued as the tarnished golden frame that embraced the beautiful Madonna on the wall. Just like the rough and curlicued Sicilian relatives embracing their newfound family visiting from far-away America.

Our departure was a repeat of our arrival. Just more of everything. There was unstoppable weeping from everyone—uncles, aunts, and even the children. There were extra kisses and extra-tight bear hugs. There were eyes filled with gratitude, pride, and tears. I was now an honest-to-God member of the Missimi *famiglia* and I was very, very proud. It would be more than 40 years before I would return to the land of my father.

THE SADDEST JOURNEY: OCTOBER 1970

It was the middle of rehearsal and things were going very well. I was directing a production of *The Me Nobody Knows* in a small studio theatre across from the campus of the University of Detroit. We were rehearsing my favorite number, "If I Had a Million Dollars," and my talented, interracial cast was circling the soloist, harmonizing the rock tune and executing the choreography with 100 percent commitment. I was so proud of their work. It was going to be a great show.

I glanced around to get the full effect of my staging when I noticed Nancy standing near the edge of the stage. She signaled to me. I tried to read her face but it was impossible to see what she was thinking. As I walked closer, I could see her tears. With no preparation she blurted out—as if she planned to say it as quickly as possible and get it over with—"Your dad died, Nick. We've got to go to New Lex."

"When?"

"Just a few hours ago. He had a heart attack."

I refused to think about it.

"Hey, everybody! Listen up." The pianist lifted his fingers and the cast turned their attention to me. "I have an emergency to take care of, so why don't you run through the musical numbers and then end early? You're really doing a great job. Thanks."

I told myself I wouldn't cry. There would be plenty of time for that once I got home. I dreaded the thought of the funeral home. It was going to be awful. Italian funerals were famous for being *una scena* from grand opera.

After a call to my sister Regina to tell her we were on our way, I grabbed an old navy-blue blazer and Nancy found a few dark items to wear for the services. As we approached Toledo, the car began to sputter. I tried to keep it going, thinking the motor eventually might solve its own problems, but soon we coasted to a stop on the side of the road. Fortunately, there were a few small businesses nearby and I hiked to a gas station to get help.

I found a place that would pick us up and fix the car. It was 10 p.m. by the time we arrived at the all-night service station. The mechanic didn't have the needed part so he couldn't fix the car for three days. We already were exhausted but had no choice except to call a taxi and head to the Toledo Greyhound station.

The first bus out was at 6 a.m. so Nancy and I cuddled on a curved wooden bench and stacked our suitcases beside us, covering ourselves with our funeral clothes to keep warm. We didn't want to say much. We were both trying to hold back the tears.

My brother Tony met us at the Columbus bus terminal and drove us to 714 North Main. I held my breath as I opened the screened door. The sad part will begin right now, I thought, as I glanced at my mother, standing in the middle of the kitchen. She came to me like a wounded child. "He's gone, Nicky. Daddy's gone." She sobbed on my shoulder and I tried desperately to hold back my tears, but it wasn't possible. Nancy and Tony joined me.

"I know, Mom. I know, I know, I know." It was all I could say. When you're family, what do you say? You can't say "He's with God now" or "God will take care of him now." Those things are what you say to someone else, someone who's not in your family. Not your mother. She just lost her husband. I just lost my dad.

Once we got mom under control, she told us what happened. He was roasting hot peppers on the gas range, something he did daily before he sat down for his meal. Mom heard a sudden crash and ran to the kitchen to find dad on the floor. He wasn't breathing. Mom screamed and my nephew Eugene ran from Regina's house next door to try to revive him, but it was useless. He had had a massive heart attack that killed him almost instantly.

The rest of our time in New Lex was a blur. There was the funeral home with the whole family in attendance, including a full contingent from Bellevue. The Italian and Lebanese neighbors paid their respects as did the townspeople who had known dad, mainly through mom's popularity and the success of his two sons. When I wasn't shaking hands and handing mom clean handkerchiefs, I took the time to study the flowers and read the many cards. The room was a veritable greenhouse. It was a nice tribute to a man who loved growing things, even if they were tomatoes, not roses.

When it was time for Tony to lead the last prayers and close the casket, I braced myself. It was the final leave-taking for the wife. I remembered many other Italian services where I became frightened at this point. My mother approached the casket.

"Oh Guy, oh Guy, I don't want to say goodbye to you!" she cried. She kissed one cheek, then the other. She grabbed his hands and kissed them and before we could stop her, she scooped her arms around him and tried to lift him from the casket. I ran to her and along with the funeral director we released dad from her grip and reverently put him back in the casket. Regina and my brother Pete steered mom out of the room as she yelled "*Madre di Dio, aiutami*!" [Mother of God, help me!])

To this day I don't know how God gave my brother Tony the strength to say the funeral Mass for his father and, later, his mother. He baptized everyone in the family, married us, and finally buried us. He gave us the thread of continuity that allowed God to be the special guest at all our most joyous and most sorrowful events.

Right after we buried dad, my mom told me something incredibly sad. We were sitting at the kitchen table having coffee and Italian cookies from Aunt Catherine. After my grandfather's death, she told me she had said to dad, "Look, Guy. For the first time in our marriage we have the house to ourselves. We don't have to take care of anyone anymore. We have our whole life to live now—together and alone!"

Two weeks later my dad lay on the kitchen floor, his hot peppers burning in the flames of the gas stove.

"I think God's mad at me," she said, with the same wounded voice that had greeted my arrival. "I must have done something wrong that made Him mad at me."

Mom was diagnosed with breast cancer soon after dad's death. She didn't seem to fight it. Whenever I visited her, she had an air of resignation. She wanted the end to come quickly. "I miss your dad," she said, her eyes welling up with tears. "I want to be with my man." In December 1972, she got her wish.

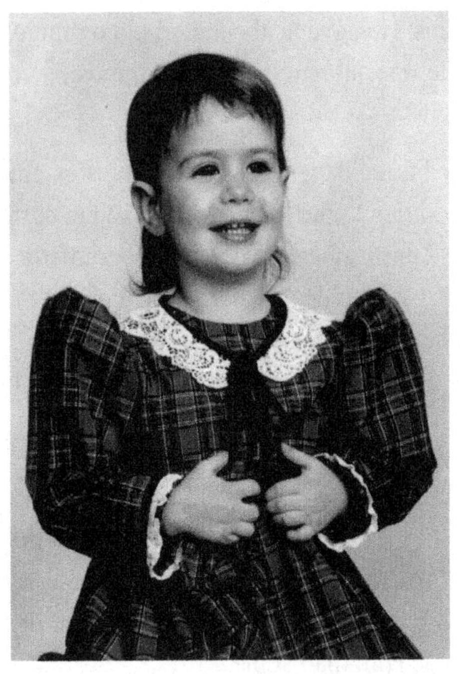

IT WAS THE BEST OF TIMES, IT WAS THE WORST OF TIMES

I'm going to start with the worst.

It was a few days before Thanksgiving and a frigid wind swept around our cozy Victorian farmhouse in North Evanston. Nancy and I had made all the preparations for this momentous day. There was a new pine crib covered in lacy, cream-colored eyelet. Hanging above the bed was a dancing mobile of delicate, hand-painted carousel horses that turned to the tune of "Love Makes the World Go Round." There was a vase of yellow daisies and purple iris on the dresser, and a new white wicker rocker for late-night baby duties. It was all perfect. We're ready—four hours until the big moment when our lives would change forever.

Then the phone rang. "Hello, Dominic?"

"Yes?"

"Oh, Dominic, it's Margaret calling from the hospital."

"Is everything okay, Margaret? Is Kristi doing all right? And the baby?"

There was an uncomfortable pause. I held my breath. "Well, I have some bad news. Is Nancy there?"

Nancy broke into the conversation somewhat breathlessly. "Yes, I'm here. I'm on the extension. What's happening?"

"Well, I'm afraid Kristi has changed her mind. One of the hospital social workers encouraged Kristi to hold her baby this morning. Once the baby was in her arms, she broke down and said she couldn't possibly give up her son. I'm so sorry. As your adoption facilitator I try to keep these things from happening, but I have no say when the birth mother wants to hold her baby. I'm so very sorry."

I have no idea what was said before we ended the call. I only know that we were thunderstruck. We had found an Italian-American birth mother through a magazine ad. As over-40 parents, we were too old to be considered by traditional adoption agencies. We supported Kristi throughout her pregnancy and had paid our facilitator to take her to her medical examinations.

We did everything people told us not to do. How could we have been so foolish? We bought the furniture, we named him Michael Anthony after our two grandfathers, and yet there we stood, next to the crib, the carousel, the rocker, and the flowers—empty handed. How would we survive this heartache, this emptiness?

But we did. Determined, we took several hundred deep breaths, closed the door to the nursery so we wouldn't see the crib, and spent the next couple of weeks searching for ways to find a child that would be ours. We promised each other from the day we learned Nancy was unable to conceive that we would be parents no matter how long it took.

A friend knew a couple who had adopted a baby from Poland. How perfect that would be! We had made every attempt to find a baby of Italian-American descent and now we would look for a child who would come from Poland, the land of my wife's ancestors. I've always loved blondes!

We were in the middle of our phone conversation with the proud parents of their new Polish baby when the mother interrupted and said, "I have something else you might be interested in."

She told us that their family doctor in South Chicago had just delivered a baby girl. Both birth parents were 15 years old. They were Irish-Catholic, and the girl's father was adamant that his daughter put her baby up for adoption. He asked the doctor to help find parents for his daughter's child. The couple gave us the doctor's phone number.

And so the miracle began and the "best of times" was at our doorstep. We called the doctor. We called our lawyer. We called the hospital to make arrangements to pick up our daughter. Was this really happening? Within two days we would drive to Saint Anthony Hospital and pick up *our* baby. We would name her Mary Elizabeth, after my grandmother and both of my wife's sisters. We decided to call her Emmy. (Originally, we'd planned on it being M.E., but since that sounded like a bank president or a forensic pathologist, we quickly changed it to Emmy.)

It was a record-breaking cold day in Chicago with a temperature of minus 2 degrees. We drove to South Chicago in silence, too overwhelmed at the prospect before us to indulge in chit-chat. The hospital staff was very courteous and treated us with amusement, knowing we were in our mid-40s and not quite typical adoptive parents. Within moments, there she was! Wrapped in her pink blankets and pink sock cap, disguising her little bald head. We both giggled as we took turns holding her and listened to the basic instructions of baby care from the nurses. And then we were on our way to our new "family" home.

I was a nervous wreck and knew I would not be a conscientious driver, so Nancy took the wheel. She cautiously drove us back to the North Shore as I sat in the back seat, buried beneath a mound of fluffy blankets and a new baby quilt that Nancy had designed and stitched for our little prize.

We won! We have our baby! Our life is complete.

Our favorite Christmas present—Emmy

Once we got her settled in her tiny room with the elegant crib, the charming carousel spinning gracefully, and a new batch of flowers giving off the scent of spring, we realized we had designed a perfect room for a little girl. It was meant to be.

After our disastrous Thanksgiving experience with Kristi and her baby, we had told no one about our latest adoption attempts. So we spent the days before Christmas calling everyone we knew.

"Hello. This is Dominic. Guess what? Nancy and I have a beautiful daughter. Her name is Emmy. We can't wait to introduce her to you!" God had smiled on us. Could there have been a more perfect Christmas gift?

JUST ONE MORE

"What do you think?" I asked.

"Yes," Nancy said, "and soon!"

And so, having settled our new daughter Emmy in her picture-perfect nursery, we made the decision to pursue another adoption. We couldn't imagine a spoiled only-child who no one could tolerate except her parents. Yes, we needed to find another child and soon—before the blush on our middle-aged cheeks turned to the sallow jowls of two old souls.

Because we couldn't pursue the standard adoption paths, we sought the help of an attorney who specialized in finding birth mothers for future parents. We found our attorney in an ad in *Parents* magazine. He seemed to be very well respected, with an excellent track record of finding babies for eager parents-to-be. Our initial meeting was productive and he promised we would have a second child in a year. The process went much faster than any of us expected and within six months he had set up a meeting with the young woman who would bring our new baby into the world.

We never met Emmy's birth mother. We only received the most basic information about her from the social worker after Emmy was born. We learned that the teenage father was the girl's good friend, the pregnancy happened on a rainy afternoon in the attic of her home, she was an average student in her Catholic high school, and her favorite class was drama. How perfect for the new parents who had spent their lives in rooms with the lights out and people pretending to be someone else. Emmy promised a life of high drama. And she has lived up to it!

Our second daughter, Angela, had a very different path into our arms. Our meeting with her mother was unforgettable, and not in a good way. A pregnant Allison, Angela's mother, arrived in the lawyer's office in downtown Chicago 15 minutes late. She was accompanied by her mother, a character who seemed as sad as she was colorful. Her hair was dyed carrot orange, perhaps owing to the fact that she was a beautician. Her most distinguishing feature was an enormous black eye, an obvious gift from one of her gentlemen friends—perhaps an angry husband or a jealous lover. Allison was in her late 20s. She came with her three young sons, who looked to be one to three. They were shabbily dressed, with soiled and smelly diapers. While Allison appeared a bit bedraggled, she was attractive and had the potential to be a "looker." But poverty and an unhappy marriage seemed to have taken its toll.

"So, Allison, tell me about your baby's father. Is he a boyfriend?"

She looked at me with disbelief. "Are you kidding me? No, he's a pig! He's the janitor in our building. He's a big, dumb Mexican!" Allison was a tough cookie.

According to the attorney, Allison's husband had given her an ultimatum—either she puts the baby up for adoption or he divorces her. She didn't have much of a choice, considering the three little screamers tearing apart the lawyer's office. When I asked about her parentage, she said she was a real "Heinz 57"—Irish, German, Croatian, and a streak of Chippewa.

"Have you ever taken drugs?" It was a bold question, but Allison's behavior was slightly edgy, and I felt the need to ask.

"Yeah," she said, "I did lots of drugs a long time ago when I was a kid, but I'm clean now. I haven't done drugs for a long time."

We shook hands with Allison and her mom, promised to keep in touch weekly, and arranged for the payment of her doctor bills and the cost of the delivery and hospital expenses.

And so we waited, our life filled with the joy of our jobs and the thrill of coming home to our beautiful little Emmy. And while we never dwelled on it, we were secretly hoping for a boy who would complete our perfect family.

In mid-July, our lawyer called to say that Allison was being taken to LaGrange Hospital. Early on the morning of July 18th he called again to tell us that Allison had delivered a beautiful baby girl, with a head full of black hair. Could we come the next day to bring the baby home?

How easy was this? Everything was like clockwork. We had the name picked out—Angela Helen, after my mother and Nancy's. We had the nursery freshened up. Emmy moved into her own tiny room, the carousel horses traveling with her across the hall. She now had a large carousel horse standing guard at the door and a parade of horses that marched around in a wallpaper border at the ceiling. Angela got an animal mobile over the cradle and a small ark with pairs of animals who now resided on top of her dresser. Everyone loves animals, whether you're a baby boy or a baby girl.

But there were complications, as we discovered upon our arrival at the hospital. When we asked to see the baby and her mother, we were told that Allison had left the hospital a few hours after she delivered Angela. Obviously, she did not want a confrontation after what we were about to find out.

"Tests reveal cocaine in Angela's urine," said the doctor. "We don't know how it has affected her. Her APGAR scores are OK, so there's no severe damage, but we'll have to watch her to determine how her mother's cocaine habit has affected little Angela."

We'd been disappointed before. But this was different. We didn't lose a baby like we did when the Italian-American girl changed her mind about giving her baby to us. We had a new baby. She was cradled in Nancy's arms and I was looking at her.

"You don't have to keep this baby," the attorney told us. "We can go back and look for a new birth mother."

"No," I said, and Nancy shook her head, too. "This is our baby. If Nancy had delivered her and if something was wrong, there would be no question. She is ours, and we'll love her for exactly who she is."

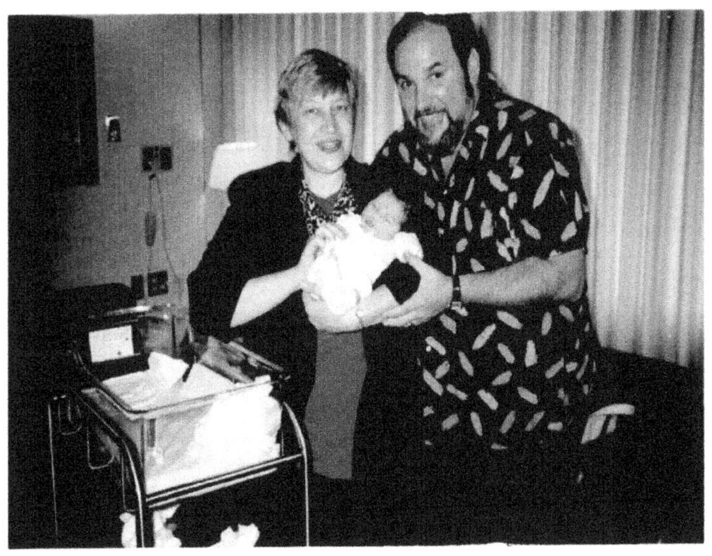

With baby Angela at the hospital

Angela was a cute and crazy-looking baby. Her hair was unusually thick, and it was spiky, as if she were a rock star from outer space—a kind of moon baby! Every time I looked at her, she made me smile.

Later, the doctors at Children's Hospital told us that, due to her mother's cocaine addiction, Angela was born with a small piece of her brain missing. In the months and years that followed, we discovered that this anomaly had no effect on her speech or movement, but her intellectual capacity was challenged. She did not have the motor skills to write clearly, nor did she have sufficient eyesight to read easily. She had difficulty with typical book-learning but had an exceptional memory, able to rattle off hundreds of song lyrics and everyone's birthdates.

While I gravitated to Emmy as Papa's little drama daughter, Nancy formed an instant bond with our little moon baby, Angela. Suddenly we had a United Nations family—a totally Italian dad Dominic, a totally Polish mom Nancy, a totally Irish daughter Emmy, and a mostly Mexican daughter Angela. *Finis*. We're set for life!

MY BROTHER, THE POPE

While my mom may have dreamed that her son Anthony would become the first American pope, I'm perfectly content with Monsignor Tony.

I never got to know Tony very well when I was growing up. He was seven years older than I, and my other siblings were even older. My two half-brothers, Louie and Pete, and my half-sister Regina seemed like grownups when I was attending grade school.

By the time I was in third grade Tony already was at Saint Aloysius Academy. I saw him only briefly between his basketball practices, play rehearsals, and many other social and school activities. The one day we actually shared the same space was

Sunday pasta dinner, which always occurred immediately following the 10:30 Mass at Saint Rose of Lima Church, where he was touted by our priest as the "perfect" server.

As a reward for all that perfection, my dad bought Tony his own little car when he was old enough to drive. It was a turquoise coupe with a homemade "vanity" license plate with his nickname—Froggy—artfully painted on it. He seemed to have everything going for him, and if we'd had a yearbook, the words "most likely to succeed" would be inscribed under his senior high school photo.

But even with the "perfect" brother, there was something missing. I wanted a brother who was closer in age to me. I wanted a brother who could be my buddy, just like all my friends who had older brothers. I had my cousin Mary. Don't get me wrong. I loved Mary like a sister, but she was a girl, and though I spent most of my high school days having her chauffeur me around town in her ancient jalopy, I never had the chance to say "screw you, asshole!" the way my friends could say to their brothers.

I wanted to go to the movies with Tony and spot him in the bleachers at my Little League games. I wanted him to treat me and my buddies to a Tasty Freeze ice cream, or share a pizza with me at Fiore's Chatterbox, or take me bowling, or fishing, or any number of things that an older brother could do. But not an older brother who was seven years older.

I remember how proud I was of him, though, when he was a member of the Ohio state championship basketball team. My parents didn't believe in attending sporting events. Actually, they didn't come to many of our activities at all. When the Saint Aloysius Academy Blue Knights of Our Lady (yes, that was our official name) made it to the championship game against Delphos St. John, the tournament was to be broadcast from the Cleveland Arena. About an hour before the start of the game I was helping my mom sweep the leaves and gravel from the patio under the grape arbor. My dad came through the screened door from the kitchen as if he were on a mission—giant strides, each step filled with purpose.

"Let's get in the car." And he headed for the 1952 Pontiac parked in the alley.

“Where are we going?” mom asked. We looked at each other with the same confusion.

“To listen to the game.”

“Well I’ll be damned!” my mom said to me with a wink.

“You mean Saint Al’s?” I asked, careful not to sound too interested. “The tournament game?”

“Yeah,” he said, “I hope you know how to find the Cleveland station.”

I hopped over the fence as mom took off her apron and threw it on our ancient Maytag washing machine pushed against the house.

“Sure,” I said, “I listen to that station all the time.” No hiding it, I was definitely interested!

And we were off to the Sunnyhill Coal Mine where we could park on one of its mini-mountains to get better reception. I still had the image of Tony as he was pictured in the sports pages of the *Zanesville Times Recorder*. He was guarding a gigantic center going up for a shot. Tony was short, but a photographer’s dream. They loved to shoot him next to players who were over a foot taller than he was. It was amazing that our high school with an enrollment of 60 boys could field a team with two players who were very tall—Bob Sagan was 6'6" and Mike Allen was an astonishing 6'8". Tony was 5'7".

So there we sat, listening intently as we heard the play-by-play broadcast. It was an intensely exciting game, and my chest swelled with pride every time I heard the announcer say his name—"and that's number 54 Tony Missimi at the foul line." A second passed. "And it's good!" I let out a yelp and my mom said, "So what happened? What's going on?"

TAKES SPILL AFTER DRIBBLE. Tony Missimi, five-foot seven-inch junior guard of New Lexington St. Aloysius' newly crowned state Class B basketball champions, is headed for a fall during the third period of St. Aloysius' 65-63 upset victory over Delphos St. John's yesterday in the Cleveland Arena. Coming up from behind the bespectabled Missimi is Ralph Elwer, St. John's senior center, hoping to regain possession of the ball.

"Tony made the point, Mom!" My dad sat in silence, confused but excited—he didn't know the rules, either. The game was a nail-biter, all the way until the final buzzer when tiny Tony Missimi and the Saint Aloysius Academy Blue Knights of Our Lady were declared State Champions, with a final score of 65-63.

I was bursting with pride. That was my big/little brother they were talking about!

I loved my brother, though I didn't know how to admit it. We never said "I love you" to anyone in our family. I'm not sure why that was. We were Italian and we were used to *tanti baci* (many kisses), double- and sometimes triple-cheeked. Maybe our moms said it to the babies, but I never heard it from parents to their kids or even from husband to wife. I thought perhaps the men felt saying "I love you" was a sign of weakness. It made them seem feminine and unmanly and their wives responded by not letting their husbands think they were too soft, too *Americano*.

Thanks to my daughter Emmy, who taught Nancy and me to say "love you" at the end of every phone conversation, I now can tell Tony I love him, and he has learned to do the same to his kid brother.

Brothers bearing gifts for the Sicilian relatives

Tony possesses all the qualities of an extraordinary human being. He never fails to be a man totally dedicated to loving. His parishioners are drawn to him because he exudes a steady glow of care and kindness. It radiates from him and you can't help but be touched by his goodness. He didn't become pope, or a cardinal, or a bishop. But he is the best little padre I could ever imagine. I love him, and I'm not embarrassed to say it.

COUSIN MARY

I spent a lot of time during high school with my cousin Mary Circelli. Our mothers were sisters, from the Apulia region in southern Italy. We were born a few months apart, lived a few houses away, and were lumped together as the neighborhood's little Italian twins. While Mary had her sister Vickey and first cousins Joann and Janet to pal around with, I had no male relatives near my age to share a day of playing catch, fishing at the reservoir, or just hanging around with a buddy. Mary was my "buddy" and it certainly had its pros and cons.

I love Mary as much as any of my immediate family. She's right up there with wife, daughters, and brother. She's still an important part of my life and as adults we make an effort to spend quality time together. As children and teenagers, however, we were inseparable.

Nick (in the driver's seat), Mary, and brother Pete. This is probably the only time I drove Mary anywhere.

Our parents never approved of most of the kids in our part of town. They were rough and a little crazy. They were even poorer than our own immigrant families and our parents insisted we stay away from the "hillbilly" kids. In actuality, we probably were considered hillbillies ourselves back in Sicily.

My mom thought farmers' and miners' kids were all dirty. And most of them were. "Stay away from those Hoops kids," my mom warned, "I hear they got lice!" Once, I sat under the grape arbor while Regina picked the nits out of Mary's and my hair. "All right, you dumb ass," my mom said affectionately, "don't you ever put someone else's hat on your head or we'll be picking those damn bugs outta your hair forever!" She had such a way with words.

The downside of hanging with Mary was that she was a girl. No matter what we fought about, she was always right, according to my mom. No matter how much Mary beat on me when we got into a quarrel, I was never right and never allowed to hit back.

"Dominic Eugene, don't you dare raise your hand to Mary! She's a girl!" my mom screamed. So while I stood in the yard trying to wrestle my baseball bat from Mary's grip, she rained down blow after blow on my back, shoulders, and legs. I had to just stand there and take it. She was a girl!

As we grew older, there were benefits to be sure. Mary was a popular high schooler. She was good looking with flashy Italian features, including dark eyes, luxurious long brown hair, and a winning smile. She also had a jalopy, which she drove around town incessantly, usually filled with the best-looking girls at St. Al's. Her passengers often included Elaine Hayden, Susie Harrison, her cousin Mary Lee Nash (my high school crush), and eventually the Nicaraguan babe, Maria Auxiliadora Conti, the most exotic boarding student at the Academy and my junior prom date. As cousin Nicky, I often was included in her carload of popularity.

Hanging out with Mary was not without its problems, though. She often asked me to help her with "girly" things like wardrobe choices, eager to model her mail-order 100-yard crinoline skirts newly arrived from a catalog company. Or she begged for advice on her latest heartthrob, such as her infatuation with Wesley Shirkey, the handsome, rough older boy whom everyone agreed was a juvenile delinquent. Witnessing the many hours I spent with Mary encouraged her father (my Uncle Phil) to tease me mercilessly for being his daughter's friend. If I accidently ran into him on the street, he would not let up.

"Well look who's here! It's Rosie O'Grady! Going shopping for a new dress, Rosie?" I was humiliated, especially if one of my guy friends was with me. Each time it happened, I swore I would never let Mary coax me into any more girl stuff. I loved cruising around town with her cute girlfriends, but I wanted to be done with the ridicule for the time I spent with her.

After our two daughters came along, Mary and I rekindled our friendship. She is my daughter Emmy's godmother and has become a close member of our family. She lives in Columbus with her son Jeff and his family—near enough to Chicago that we can get together regularly.

She had a long and rewarding career as a staff photographer for the *Columbus Dispatch* and her work has won many awards.

Though she was a great photographer, what has impressed me most about Mary as an adult is the *hutzpah* she showed in standing up to the paper and demanding equal pay for women journalists. She won her case and became a role model for professional journalistic photographers. I guess all the beatings she gave me as a kid were good preparation for her getting down and dirty with employers who needed to be taught a lesson.

We always could count on Mary to be the official photographer at our reunions, pulling out the camera to document our family history as it happened. As a result, we have hundreds of great photos taken over the years.

In Tuscany (Piazza Garibaldi, Cortona)

One of the special joys of our renewed friendship has been traveling together. We've taken six trips to Italy thus far—with long stays in Tuscany, Rome, Ischia, and Apulia, where our grandparents were born, and in Sicily to visit my father's family. We've had fantastic adventures, with me holding the maps and Mary negotiating her way on and off the Italian autostradas. She hates reading maps and I hate driving, so it has worked out perfectly.

I am so grateful that Mary has been in my life. She is more than a cousin—she is my sister. Nothing makes me happier than the thought that we've been able to enjoy each other's company, and lives, for more than 70 years.

SUNRISE, SUNSET

I have two more years to live. That's what one of America's most respected oncologists told me. "You have a very serious form of cancer. Removing the tumor requires a difficult surgery and many patients don't survive."

I thought my visit to the doctor at Northwestern University Hospital would be relatively straightforward. I had planned to say, "Set a date for the surgery and I'll go home and tell my wife and kids." Instead, I was sitting there facing the doctor as tears ran down my cheeks. How will I tell my family? As I surveyed the pale green office my eyes landed on a piece of art hanging on the wall. It was a dazzling sunset (or sunrise—it was impossible to tell) and an empty road. How ironic, I thought.

I couldn't accept the prognosis. The thought of telling my family I would be gone in a couple of years was something I could not fathom. I had tortured myself occasionally with imagining the loss of my wife and children—a slip on the ice for Nancy and a fatal head injury, a late-night car accident with Emmy and her friends, or Angela's sudden dash into the street and an unseen speeding car. This was my actor's imagination working overtime.

I immediately sought a second opinion and made arrangements to meet with Stephen Sener, MD, at Evanston Hospital. He is among the country's leading cancer surgeons and a specialist in duodenal cancer, my disease. It is treated in the same manner as pancreatic cancer, often having the same deadly results.

"We'll fix you," the doctor said. "We'll do the Whipple procedure, which I think will be the best way to deal with it." Because of the difficult location of the tumor, "the Whipple" provided a path for the surgeon to find and remove it—along with my gall bladder, a large portion of my pancreas, and parts of my intestines. It definitely messed with my plumbing, but I had faith in the surgeon, who had a great track record with this type of operation.

I hated hospitals. I had spent only a few days in a hospital when I was 13 and had a severe bout of pneumonia and complications from mumps. Remember that story about the testicles? It was no laughing matter, really, as I could have become sterile.

The surgery went well. Dr. Sener was pleased with the results and felt confident I would make a good recovery. It was a matter of how my body would react to all the tinkering with my internal organs.

The first few days in the hospital, I was inundated with bizarre sensory experiences. My room was a greenhouse with dozens of flower arrangements from family and colleagues. But it wasn't the flowers that assaulted my senses. Rather, it was the overwhelming scent of floral perfume worn by the Filipino nurses who constantly bustled in and out to check my vitals. I thought perfume was forbidden for nurses and caregivers. Or had all the drugs triggered some other sensory overloads? Was I imagining the intense fragrance of gardenias, lilacs, and roses?

One night, I had a reaction to a sleep drug. I awoke, glanced down, and appeared to be lying on a bier. An almost-see-through gray gauze covered me. It was draped over my face but through it I could see the cold, white lights shining down on me. It's my shroud, I thought. I've died. And I began to weep. Slowly, I drifted out of my stupor. I had to find out if I was dead or alive. I called Nancy and told her about the shroud. "You're fine, Dominic. You're just a little high on your drugs."

I came home two weeks after the surgery and began my regimen of chemo treatments and runny creamed soups. I had nothing to complain about, though. I was getting stronger day by day and, most important of all, I was alive.

It has been more than 10 years since my surgery. I occasionally am tempted to call that doctor at Northwestern University

Hospital and encourage her to meet Robert Sener, MD, and exchange a few ideas about duodenal cancer. Dr. Sener was my savior and it was proven every time I went for medical exams and encountered other physicians. They always said "You're one of the lucky ones! Not many people survive 'the Whipple.'" This became even more apparent when a very good friend, a talented musician and composer, was diagnosed with duodenal cancer, had "the Whipple" surgery, and died within a few months.

With every sunrise I thank God that He has given me the gift of my wife and daughters. But most of all, He gave me the precious time to be with them as I move into my "sunset" years. At my last visit to my oncologist she said, "You're good. You don't have to come back again for a CT scan. I think you're done with cancer." That was the news I wanted to hear and believe—and it was a decade in the making! *Grazie, Dio*!

THE THINGS I LOVE

I love Puccini operas at the Met, seeing Broadway shows with my daughter Emmy, cheering the Cubbies in the bleachers at Wrigley Field, cruising down Lake Shore Drive with the Chicago skyline in front of me, but most of all, I love eating. To be more specific, I love eating Italian food.

At the top of my favorite-food list is pasta. I cannot exist without pasta. Even when my doctor tells me to lay off the noodles to help keep my glucose numbers down, I can't pass it up. Everyone in my family, including me, has a history of diabetes and cardiovascular disease: all four grandparents, mom and dad, my brothers Louis and Pete, and sister Regina. Only my priestly brother Tony was spared.

A lifetime of pasta has taken its toll. I've always been astounded to see the slim-hipped, paunch-less men walking around the piazzas in Italy. Somehow, I've never made the Mediterranean diet work for me. Worst of all, Italian-Americans, including me, seem to have forgotten the sensible portions served at an Italian meal.

While I am a major fan of standard pastas like spaghetti, mostaccioli, rigatoni, fettuccini, rotini, orecchiette, farfalle, and the dozens of other varieties, I've always had a soft spot in my heart (what a terrible thing to say!) for stuffed pastas like ravioli, cannelloni, and Sicilian shells. I also have great respect for any cook who can create light, pillowy gnocchi, so different from the leaden and gummy store-bought varieties. Nothing, and I mean nothing, is as satisfying for me as pasta with plain tomato-based sauce, tons of garlic and basil, sprinkled with lots of *parmigiano*. That's a plate of Italian heaven.

I think that is what often impresses American tourists when they sit down in an Italian trattoria for a plate of pasta. Simplicity. Fantastically fresh ingredients, and only a few. On the less healthy side, I also would not mind dying from a creamy, cheesy Alfredo or a fragrant pesto sauce. Then there's carbonara. Those Romans know how to make magic with bacon and eggs!

It may sound a bit peculiar, but I love flowers. Even as a kid I eagerly crossed the street to look at the flower seed packets on the porch of the Jack Sprat Valley Market. I was amazed by the miracle of planting zinnia and marigold seeds on a warm April day, watching them pop up in May, and seeing them stand tall in June and July. We had dozens of wild rose bushes growing against our broken-down wire fence, along with enormous lilacs. Passing through our yard was a huge olfactory celebration. I gathered large bouquets of these spring flowers to place on the May altar to the Blessed Mother in my bedroom. I didn't care that my mom yelled at me, "You and those damn flowers—you're gonna bring ants inta the house!"

And Easter! The sidewalk in front of Hatem's Confectionary was a carpet of flowers. Enormous pots of hydrangeas, all sizes of red clay pots filled with brilliant-colored tulips, white and yellow jonquils, and dozens of containers of white lilies, just like the ones that dressed the nave of the church, filling the space with the sweetest scent—the fragrance of death and resurrection.

To this day, I'm thrilled when my senses are tickled with the sight and smell of food or flowers. Some of my best flower experiences have been in Italy. What can match the Tuscan hills when there is an unbroken carpet of red, red poppies or the brilliant golden yellow of endless sunflowers? It takes my breath away.

I'm equally dazzled by the riot of colors at the Italian *mercati* (markets), the fantastic flower stands throughout Europe, and the tiny New York bodegas filling city sidewalks with cascades of blossoms.

I'm envious of people who can afford to have fresh flowers in their homes every day. I try. I buy my three bouquets for $12 at the local supermarket, almost always with Stargazer lilies because

they intoxicate me with their unique and overpowering scent. I know lots of people hate them. It's as overwhelming as that intrusive tea-rose perfume I associate with wealthy dowagers. But it satisfies my soul and I've often told my daughter Emmy that I want them at my funeral.

I also love classical ballet. This obsession may have started after I saw the great Russian ballet companies when I reviewed their performances for the *Varsity News* at the University of Detroit. Physical beauty and athleticism, theatrical magic, and magnificent music were the ingredients that made me a life-long balletomane. I love the sublime beauty of male and female bodies moving in perfect harmony as they stretch, jump, turn, and fill the space with kinetic wonder.

My love of dance led to the creation of a dance major at the University of Detroit and a ballet company called DANCE DETROIT in the early 1970s. I produced, and my students performed, the Detroit Symphony Orchestra's first fully staged production of *The Nutcracker.*

To help my male acting students at U of D become more aware of their movement potential, I drove a carload of them out to the 'burbs every Saturday to a small regional ballet company,

Michigan Ballet Theatre. I joined them for weekly classes. We must have been a pitiful sight those first few months in our baggy tights and ill-fitting ballet slippers, but eventually we joined their *corps de ballet* in performance. I even appeared as Dr. Drosselmeyer in their *Nutcracker*, partnering a remarkable young dancer, Karen Ziemba, a triple-threat performer who became a Tony-winning Broadway star.

In 1971 I had my greatest experience as a balletomane. Nancy and I were on our year-long overseas sabbatical, during which we attended performances in Great Britain and on the continent by the world's greatest ballet companies.

But one evening stands out—the most glorious time I ever spent in a theatre. It was at the Royal Opera House in Covent Garden, long before London's famed flower and vegetable market became gentrified and turned into a major tourist attraction. We saw a performance of Prokofiev's *Romeo and Juliet*, danced by the prima ballerina of the Royal Ballet, Margot Fonteyn. She was partnered by the newly defected and universally adored Rudolf Nureyev. It was highly anticipated. She was elegant in her mid-40s and he was a virtuosic, wild-haired Russian in his 20s. She was dancing the role of a 13-year-old girl—Juliet Capulet.

What happened on that stage was a miracle. It was the balcony scene that ended the first act and it counts as the most exciting half-hour of my theatre-going life (and I have seen thousands of hours of performances in hundreds of theatres throughout the world).

Nureyev and Fonteyn in Romeo and Juliet

The beauty of live dance performance is that, sometimes, something inexplicable occurs. It's what many dance critics label "beyond technique." It's when all the standard steps of the ballet vocabulary morph into an almost out-of-body experience. Fonteyn and Nureyev were executing all the steps choreographer Kenneth MacMillan had given them, but they were possessed by their roles. They were drawn to each other with some kind of magnetic force that made them one. Their commitment to the characterizations turned them into special vessels of dance. They seemed to turn endlessly, and Nureyev jumped higher than seemed possible. Their lifts and balances were perfection.

As an audience, we sat in a trance—unable to breathe. All we could do was look upon the most beautiful depiction of love ever.

It was beyond "beyond." When the curtain fell, as Juliet reached down from her balcony and extended her hand to her handsome Romeo, the audience sat stunned. What did we just see? We came to the same conclusion at the exact same moment, because the audience exploded. We couldn't believe the perfection we had just witnessed! We clapped and clapped, and they bowed and bowed and flowers showered down from the high balconies. We would not let them leave the stage. It was a 15-minute ovation. We didn't want an intermission, we wanted to stay with them and pay tribute to the most beautiful dancing we might ever see in our lives.

But ballet isn't always perfect. That same year, on our way to visit my relatives in Sicily, Nancy and I stumbled upon a performance of Stravinsky's *The Firebird* at an outdoor theatre in Lyon. We were excited to attend and to have a rest stop before we continued on our way.

The ballet began and disaster struck. The Firebird entered, *bourree-ing en pointe* (fast, rhythmic dancing on the toes of the pointe shoes) across the stage, but as soon as she stopped the movement, her feet flew out from under her and she landed on her butt with a thud. Everyone in the audience let out a gasp. She got up with as much dignity and elegance as she could muster, but when she attempted to execute the next step she did a belly-smacker, sliding across the stage with arms and legs spread out like a child's imitation of an airplane.

She stood and inched cautiously to the side of the stage, each step placed carefully, as if she really was walking on eggs. With eyes glazed, she stared into the wings and escaped as inconspicuously as she could. Unfortunately, it was time for the entrance of the *corps de ballet.* The next 30 seconds of choreography was a brilliant bit of slapstick tragedy, befitting the most ridiculous scenes from a Three Stooges movie. Nothing could save the company of dancers as they slipped and slid across the black linoleum floor, colliding and piling up on various parts of the stage. An early dew had settled, and unbeknownst to the stage crew or the dancers, the floor had become a skating rink.

The dancers crawled off the stage, the performance was cancelled, and we received a refund. But it seemed that the two minutes we had witnessed was worth the price of admission. Watching a group of magnificently trained dancers careening across the stage like a class of rollicking preschoolers seemed preposterous. How sad to think of Stravinsky's *Firebird* as one of the funniest theatrical performances we had ever seen.

The Missimi family with Bellevue relatives

AND ONE MORE THING

One has to stop somewhere. As I wrap up this "guided autobiography," I'm reminded of so many people I still want to talk about. Here are some very special ones.

George Sagan was my high school buddy, a teenager totally different from his Italian friend, Nick. How could I have picked as a friend a guy who couldn't wait to skip school for the first day of hunting season? And yet, for all our differences, we were easy friends, tooling around New Lex in his car night after night, looking for our pals to meet up at the D&B Restaurant for a smoke and a burger before we headed home. Sadly, George died too soon, in 2011, at the age of 67.

At the University of Detroit, I met another close friend, Don Powell, now a Dominican priest, Father Matthew. The minute I arrived on campus our classmates insisted that the two Italians from Ohio should meet. Don's family was from Springfield, Ohio, and his surname was Paoletti, typically changed by his grandparents to fit better into their new country. We had the same Ohio twang and shared hundreds of nights grabbing midnight snacks at Temple's, an off-campus greasy spoon, and working on our new musical, *Waterloo*. The show was set in a small Midwestern town at the "Waterloo Military Academy," modeled on St. Al's but with older boys. We were sure it was destined for Broadway, though neither of us could write a note of music. Matthew now lives in the priory at Providence College in Rhode Island, where he is on the theatre faculty. I don't see him nearly as much as I would like. He hates to travel and spends most of his time writing and working on his massive collection of crèches, the mostly Neapolitan statues of the Holy Family and a colorful cast of characters surrounding baby Jesus in the manger. Matthew has published a beautiful coffee table book, *The Christmas Crèche: Treasure of Faith, Art, and Theater.*

It was also at U of D that I became the best of friends with Robert Janosik, with whom I shared an apartment for two years and who served as best man at my wedding. Bob was a talented artist, actor, and scholar, earning a law degree from the University of Chicago and a Ph.D. in politics from NYU. Ten years after his graduation he contracted AIDS and died in a Pasadena hospital, not far from Occidental College where he taught during the last years of his life. I traveled to California to say my goodbyes to him. It was a tragic end for such an exceptional human being, such an extraordinary friend, and it was an enormous loss for me.

I also want to recognize two friends who were constant supports for me during my career at Northwestern. James Kall was one of my first students. I spent many hours sitting at the bar in the college dive where Jim served as bartender. He was my sounding board—someone to complain to, feed me the gossip regarding my new batch of students, and shoot the breeze with. He continues to be a wonderful friend to Nancy and me.

Fred Klaisner was the University's Director of Alumni Relations for national clubs. Fred introduced himself to me shortly after I directed my first big musical at NU, *Pippin*. He asked me to direct a traveling musical revue for our national alumni chapters across the country. This began a friendship of two decades of road-tripping with talented students and with Fred as our producer. As I learned more about Fred's interest in theatre, I welcomed him as my directorial assistant, and we tackled several professional productions together in Chicago. I was so proud of him when he eventually landed the job of stage manager for the national touring company of *The Lion King*.

Jim and Fred stood by me when Nancy and I adopted our two children, always the proud uncles to Emmy and Angela and best friends to their father.

My "Bellevue family," as my mom often referred to them, includes the incredibly kind aunts and uncles and their children who, like my father, came from the hilltowns surrounding Sant'Agata di Militello in Sicily and settled in Bellevue, Ohio.

They lived very close to my grandparents Tony and Maria Missimi, as if they were re-creating their Sicilian village. We only saw them twice a year—once when we made our annual summer trip to Bellevue and once when they came to New Lex.

Two of Grandpa and Grandma Missimi's children followed their parents to America—Uncle Jim and Aunt Catherine.

Uncle Jim was my dad's brother. His given name was Vincenzo but was bastardized by an immigration officer who decided that it translated to "Jim." He was married to a tiny, saintly, ever-smiling woman, Aunt Leonilda (Linda), who melted my heart every time she said, "God blessa you Neeky." I have had a close relationship with their daughter Rose, who married and returned to live in Sicily with her husband, Cologero Pidala. With my brother Tony and cousin Mary we visited Rose at her home in the hilltown of Longi. An unforgettable trip.

Lunch with Cousin Rose and her family in Longi, Sicily

Aunt Catherine came to America in the 1950s, returned to Sicily to marry Uncle Rosario Piscitello, and came back to Bellevue to begin her family. She was kindness personified and a spectacular cook, as were all the women of my "Bellevue family."

Over the years I have become very close with Aunt Catherine's daughter Rita, who has often invited Tony, Mary, and me to her house for Christmas-cookie-baking sessions with wonderful recipes handed down from her mother. From the time I was a young boy, I eagerly looked forward to the annual arrival of Aunt Catherine's Christmas cookies, always shipped in a shoe box, and when we were lucky, in a boot box. Now, Rita has taken up the cookie cutter. She continues the traditions and qualities of her mother and my mother, a never-ending supply of kindness and hospitality.

Cousins Rita and Mary and Aunt Linda baking for Christmas

These are my favorite Italian cookies, from an old Sicilian recipe adapted by my Aunt Catherine Piscitello. Her two daughters, Rita Rohlf and Mary Close, continue the tradition of Christmas cookie-baking. Warning: this recipe makes a lot of cookies!

Aunt Catherine's Tu Tu Chocolate Cookies

5 cups flour
6 eggs
3/4 cup cocoa
1/2 lb Crisco
3 cups sugar
2 cups water
1 Tbsp cinnamon
3/4 cup nuts
2 Tbsp baking powder
heaping 1/4 cup raisins

Cream together eggs, Crisco, sugar, cocoa, baking powder, and cinnamon. Add flour, nuts, raisins, and water and mix together thoroughly. Roll into small balls and place on greased cookie sheet or cookie sheet lined with parchment paper. Bake at 350 for 15 minutes.

For frosting, blend 2 lbs powdered sugar and 1 Tbsp Crisco. Add enough milk until frosting becomes thicker than a glaze but still thick enough to cover cookies.

Our Bellevue aunts and uncles have passed away. Rita is our connection now to our Sicilian roots, even though we have been thoroughly “Americanized” since our relatives first stepped onto Ellis Island to begin their new life in America.

I know there are many others. But one has to stop somewhere.

So, a final word, *Grazie*!

The Dominic Missimi Family

A LEGACY LETTER TO MY FAMILY

IT'S A WONDERFUL LIFE

I recently learned about legacy letters. They are intended to convey one's personal values, life lessons, hopes and blessings, apologies and thank-yous—and love—to family and friends.

It's a Wonderful Life—the perfect opener for this legacy letter. Thank you, Frank Capra, for creating this monumental Christmas film with its message that extends far beyond the season of frozen bridges and tinkling bells.

I never have faced the same obstacles as poor George Bailey, the movie's central character, but I have shared the joys that helped save our hero from destruction. George learned from his guardian angel Clarence that, in the end, your reward is what you give to others.

I am certain that like my own parents, most of us have been taught this same important lesson. So I write this letter as a reminder to my two children, Emmy and Angela, that you should continue to practice the "giving" virtues. Love. Charity. Kindness. Love your family, be generous to those less fortunate, be kind to everyone, always do your best, and love God.

My *vita bella* has been made up of countless small, unforgettable pieces in the crazy quilt of my life with you, Emmy and Angela.

Emmy, I'm thinking about all those horrible Thursday afternoons when Nancy was at work, laughing and crying as I desperately tried to arrange your hair for your ballet class. How do I make a bun? How do I use hairpins? What a disastrous hairdresser I was! These days, there's more laughing and crying whenever you bring me a new favorite YouTube video—the dog talking through its bark, the chatty woman wildly slapping her itchy Afro, and the worst-ever high-school rendition of "One Day More" from *Les Mis.* To this day we fall down laughing at all the absurd moments we've shared together.

How can I ever forget the day I lost you, Angela? I was absent-mindedly planting impatiens in the front yard as you rode your tricycle. Little did I know that you were pedaling from home to the Northwestern University campus. An hour later, after dozens of neighbors and friends had combed the north end of Evanston (even Emmy on her bike with a posse of friends), a police car pulled up in front of our house. We held our breath. "We found her 15 blocks from here," said the officer. It was a miracle. You, our special-needs treasure, had crossed a half-dozen major streets while your guardian angel kept you safe and brought you home to us in a police car. "Hi Mom," you said, jumping out. "I went for a ride." We gave you the biggest hugs ever, Angelina Ballerina.

In many legacy letters, the writers often leave special and significant items to family members. Instead, I ask you, Emmy and Angela, to give *me* a few significant items, but only on loan.

Since Emmy was a year old, she has been attached to a small, stuffed animal we gave her on our first visit to Florida—a flamingo called "Pinky." Angela has an equally tattered koala that she calls "Mr. Moon." She still takes Mr. Moon to bed with her. I want these two precious toys to keep me company during my days in the funeral home. Somewhere close to me so that my spirit can be comforted by their presence. I want to be connected to those perfect days when Nancy and I were in love with life because of the two remarkable gifts that had been given to us—you girls.

God has blessed me with a charmed life. He has given me a wife of 50-plus years and two daughters who have grown into kind and loving women. I hope the ribbon that has tied all these things together—love, respect, and friendship—will encircle you, my dear family, and keep us bound together forever.

THE FINAL CURTAIN

My creative imagination can be both a blessing and a curse. When I'm about to stage a Mozart opera or a Shakespeare comedy, I unleash my imagination and dream up fantastically inventive concepts for the production, filled with flowers, rainbow confetti, tambourines, and maybe a clown or two. But when I send my imagination in the opposite direction, I find I'm drifting down a shadowy path, waltzing to a *danse macabre*, fantasizing about how I might stage my final curtain.

Like watching the world walk by me in my casket....

At the funeral home, the casket is the best seat in the house. Well, not quite a seat, but I certainly have the best sight lines—plus, it's comfortable. Of course, I'm all over the room, checking on the guests (just as I did for my mom's many "under the arbor" gatherings). I'm at the door watching people sign the guest book. I'm standing behind my wife and daughters seated near the casket. I'm glued to my older brother Tony, a Catholic priest who has baptized every baby in our family and married and buried all of us, just like he'll do with me tomorrow morning. He's in his 90s, and though he'll need a little help getting up the altar steps, I have no doubt he's written a nice tribute for his kid brother. How fortunate that God gave the Missimi famiglia *this special angel.*

Nancy called Emmy three days ago at 8:30 a.m. "Hey, honey. I'm going to say this fast." (That's exactly what she said when she told me my dad had died.) "Your dad passed away in his sleep. Please come as soon as you can."

I died during the night—heart attack, they said—but maybe I was just really, really tired. It's not how I thought it would be. I always thought Nancy would precede me since she has had health issues all her life, especially during the past several years as she endured the pains of post-polio syndrome and major spine surgery. But there she is. As blonde as the day I married her. Her mother had totally white hair when she was 60, but Nancy still looks like the very blonde Mary Travers from Peter, Paul and Mary.

She's sitting quietly. I don't think she'll cry until the end. She's a strong woman. But I think Emmy will get her going, as she gets very emotional every time one of my former students comes over to offer sympathy.

There's a recording of Pachelbel's "Canon" playing softly in the room. Emmy can't help but remember that this was the music we chose for walking down the aisle together at her wedding. This was our song. She's crying. I'd also like to cry, shed a tear or two, but I don't want to scare my cousin Rita, who's kneeling in front of me. Besides, I haven't figured out that trick yet.

My special-needs daughter Angela is watching the hubbub around her. She seems to enjoy all the attention and the family reunion party vibe. I don't think she totally understands what death is. She knows "Dog" is lying in a box but I'm not sure she realizes I won't be visiting her at her group home next week. (In our family-nickname shorthand, I am "Dog," Nancy is "Cat," Emmy is "Pup," and Angela is "Kitten.")

There's a long line waiting to offer condolences. Many of my old friends from Northwestern are here, as are a number of professional actors, most of whom were former students. And of course, there's family. My brothers' and sister's children are here. Next to them are my cousin Mary and her family, including her grandkids. Sitting next to grandson Jake is his beautiful, perfectly dressed girlfriend. This must make Mary very happy, even on a day I know she's very sad. How I'll miss her!

I've drawn a nice crowd. I'd say a full house, maybe even SRO, though that's hard to gauge in a funeral home parlor. It's a pleasant room—very tasteful, with classic traditional furniture. And the dozens of flower arrangements add a rather spectacular garden element, which is a special treat since I've made my exit in early December and I've always loved flowers. I'm glad Nancy and Emmy requested the florist to put some Stargazer lilies into the spray on the coffin. I know some people hate their overpowering scent, but I love it. To me it always has been "eau de funeral home" but I find the fragrance euphoric.

The music has switched to Josh Groban singing in Italian from the movie Il Postino. *I hope Emmy has had good luck arranging music for the funeral tomorrow. I'm looking forward to a string quartet for Samuel Barber's "Adagio for Strings." And one of my favorite students, Tony-winner Heather Headley, singing "Home" from* The Wiz. *I melt the minute I hear her gorgeous voice singing the first line, "When I think of home, I think about a place where there's love overflowing." I want that to be the perfect description of my big day tomorrow.*

Two small, stuffed animals sit by my hands—Emmy's "Pinky" and Angela's "Mr. Moon." I asked both girls to let me borrow their special friends to keep me company while I'm here.

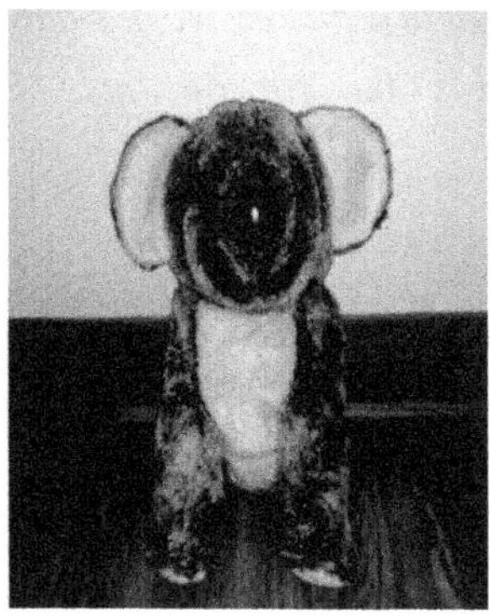

Pinky and Mr. Moon

In about 30 minutes Tony will lead the rosary. I know it's really unfashionable, but I asked for it. It's a tribute to my Italian heritage. I love its repetition. It's a kind of "keening" that gives me comfort. I remember all those old Italian women at family funerals who could speak the prayers so rhythmically and with such a regular tempo that you became mesmerized by the rhythm of the Hail Marys.

I'm whispering to Nancy, Emmy, and Angela right now. Breathing softly on their necks. I'm hoping they'll know I'm there with them. (Another trick.) I want Emmy to look at her mother, and she does. "I think I smell dad's cologne. Acqua de Gio. Can you smell it?"

Nancy looks at her. "You know I can't smell anything. Never have." But she inhales deeply anyway. She looks at me and then at Emmy, her eyes filled with disbelief. "I think I smell him." I want to change my peaceful, frozen expression to a smile so she can see that I made it happen. Perhaps that trick will come in time. After all, it's only been a few days, and I have an eternity of days to learn all the ways I can talk to them—"I love you, and I will always be with you. Just watch for the signs!"

IMAGE CREDITS

Cover by Tony Andrade

Family trees on pages 7 and 8 by Geoffrey Edwards

Back cover map and manuscript illustrations on pages 14 and 68 by Gerry Pearson Nichols

Photos of St. Rose of Lima Elementary School nuns on page 92 courtesy of Archives of the Sisters of Saint Francis of Holy Name Province, Inc., Stella Niagara, NY 14144

Photo of *Buon Natale* banner on page 97 courtesy of Anyoccasionbanners

Composite photo on page 123 by Jennifer Girard

Photo of "Oklahoma Morning Road" on page 176 by Mike Robinson

Photo of Nureyev and Fonteyn on page 185 by Roger Wood © Royal Opera House / ArenaPAL

Made in the USA
Monee, IL
06 June 2021